CHEMISTRY

CLEP* Study Guide

All rights reserved. This Study Guide, Book and Flashcards are protected under the US Copyright Law. No part of this book or study guide or flashcards may be reproduced, distributed or stored in a retrieval system, or transmitted in any form or by any means, electronic, mechanical, photocopying, recording, or otherwise, without the prior written permission of the publisher Breely Crush Publishing, LLC.

© 2019 Breely Crush Publishing, LLC

*CLEP is a registered trademark of the College Entrance Examination Board which does not endorse this book.

971091218143

Copyright ©2003 – 2019, Breely Crush Publishing, LLC.

All rights reserved.

This Study Guide, Book and Flashcards are protected under the US Copyright Law. No part of this publication may be reproduced, distributed or stored in a retrieval system, or transmitted in any form or by any means, electronic, mechanical, photocopying, recording, or otherwise, without the prior written permission of the publisher Breely Crush Publishing, LLC.

Published by Breely Crush Publishing, LLC
10808 River Front Parkway
South Jordan, UT 84095
www.breelycrushpublishing.com

ISBN-10: 1-61433-561-3
ISBN-13: 978-1-61433-561-0

Printed and bound in the United States of America.

*CLEP is a registered trademark of the College Entrance Examination Board which does not endorse this book.

Table of Contents

Atomic Theory and Atomic Structure 1
Periodic Properties 3
Chemical Bonding 5
Compounds 10
Naming Compounds 11
The Mole Concept 12
Percent Composition and Empirical Formula 14
Gases 15
Gas Laws 16
Liquids and Solids 17
Phase Changes 19
Solutions 20
Concentrations – Molarity, Molality, and Normality 21
Colligative Properties 22
Acids and Bases 23
pH and pOH 24
Precipitates 25
Common Ion Effect and Buffers 25
Writing Equations for Chemical Reactions 25
Predicting Reactions: Reaction Types 26
Balancing Chemical Equations 27
Stoichiometry 27
Limiting Reagent 29
Theoretical Yield, Actual Yield, and Percent Yield 30
Oxidation-Reduction Equations and Net Ionic Equations 30
Half-cell Potentials 32
Gibbs Free Energy, Enthalpy and Entropy 33
Equilibrium 35
Reaction Rates and Rate Laws 35
Organic Chemistry 37
Nuclear Chemistry 39
About Sample Test Questions 41
Sample Test Questions 41
Test Taking Strategies 72
What Your Score Means 72
Test Preparation 73
Legal Note 73

Periodic Table of the Elements

1A																	0
1 H Hydrogen 1.01	2A											3A	4A	5A	6A	7A	2 He Helium 4.00
3 Li Lithium 6.94	4 Be Beryllium 9.01											5 B Boron 10.81	6 C Carbon 12.01	7 N Nitrogen 14.01	8 O Oxygen 16.00	9 F Fluorine 18.00	10 Ne Neon 20.18
11 Na Sodium 22.99	12 Mg Magnesium 24.31	3B	4B	5B	6B	7B	8B	8B	8B	1B	2B	13 Al Aluminum 28.98	14 Si Silicon 28.09	15 P Phosphorus 30.97	16 S Sulfur 32.06	17 Cl Chlorine 35.45	18 Ar Argon 39.95
19 K Potassium 39.10	20 Ca Calcium 40.08	21 Sc Scandium 44.96	22 Ti Titanium 47.90	23 V Vanadium 50.94	24 Cr Chromium 52.00	25 Mn Manganese 54.94	26 Fe Iron 55.85	27 Co Cobalt 58.93	28 Ni Nickel 58.71	29 Cu Copper 63.55	30 Zn Zinc 65.38	31 Ga Gallium 69.72	32 Ge Germanium 72.59	33 As Arsenic 74.92	34 Se Selenium 78.96	35 Br Bromine 79.90	36 Kr Krypton 83.80
37 Rb Rubidium 85.47	38 Sr Strontium 87.62	39 Y Yttrium 88.91	40 Zr Zirconium 91.22	41 Nb Niobium 92.91	42 Mo Molybdenum 95.94	43 Tc Technecium (99)	44 Ru Ruthenium 101.07	45 Rh Rhodium 102.91	46 Pd Palladium 106.42	47 Ag Silver 107.87	48 Cd Cadmium 112.41	49 In Indium 114.82	50 Sn Tin 118.69	51 Sb Antimony 121.75	52 Te Tellurium 127.60	53 I Iodine 126.90	54 Xe Xenon 131.30
55 Cs Cesium 132.91	56 Ba Barium 137.34	71 Lu Lutetium 174.97	72 Hf Hafnium 178.49	73 Ta Tantalum 180.95	74 W Tungsten 183.85	75 Re Rhenium 186.21	76 Os Osmium 190.20	77 Ir Iridium 192.22	78 Pt Platinum 195.09	79 Au Gold 196.97	80 Hg Mercury 200.59	81 Tl Thallium 204.37	82 Pb Lead 207.19	83 Bi Bismuth 208.98	84 Po Polonium 209	85 At Astatine 210	86 Rn Radon (222)
87 Fr Francium (223)	88 Ra Radium 226.03	103 Lr Lawrencium (260)	104 Rf Rutherfordium (257)	105 Db Dubnium (260)	106 Sg Seaborgium 263	107 Bh Bohrium (262)	108 Hs Hassium (265)	109 Mt Meitnerium (266)	110 Ds Darmstadtium (271)	111 (272)	112 (277)	113	114 (296)	115	116 (298)	117	118 (300)

57 La Lanthanum 138.91	58 Ce Cerium 140.12	59 Pr Praseodymium 140.91	60 Nd Neodymium 144.24	61 Pm Promethium (145)	62 Sm Samarium 150.40	63 Eu Europium 151.96	64 Gd Gadolinium 157.25	65 Tb Terbium 158.93	66 Dy Dysprosium 162.50	67 Ho Holmium 164.93	68 Er Erbium 167.26	69 Tm Thulium 168.93	70 Yb Ytterbium 173.04
89 Ac Actinium (227)	90 Th Thorium (232)	91 Pa Protactinium 231.04	92 U Uranium 238.03	93 Np Neptunium 237.05	94 Pu Plutonium (244)	95 Am Americium (243)	96 Cm Curium (247)	97 Bk Berkelium (247)	98 Cf Californium (251)	99 Es Einsteinium (254)	100 Fm Fermium (257)	101 Md Mendelevium (258)	102 No Nobilium (259)

Color Key:
- s electrons
- d electrons
- p electrons
- f electrons

Atomic Theory and Atomic Structure

The Theory of Atoms was proposed in 1808 by John Dalton:

1. Each element is made up of tiny particles called **atoms**.
2. The atoms of a given element are identical; the atoms of different elements are different in some fundamental way or ways.
3. Chemical compounds are formed when atoms combine with each other. A given compound always has the same relative numbers and types of atoms.
4. Chemical reactions involve reorganization of the atoms – changes in the way they are bound together. The atoms themselves are not changed in a chemical reaction.

Atoms are composed of **protons** and **neutrons** in the nucleus, providing the mass of the atom. Protons are positively charged particles and neutrons are neutral. Early work in electricity helped with the discovery of **electrons**, negatively charged particles with 2000 times less mass than hydrogen and 1840 times less mass than either protons or neutrons. (Each proton and neutron is composed of three quarks). The electrons surround the nucleus in a sort of cloud.

The **atomic number** of an element is the number of protons it has. In an atom, the number of electrons equals the number of protons so that the atom has no charge. Its **mass number** is the actual number of protons plus neutrons in the nucleus. **Isotopes** are atoms of the same element so they have the same number of protons, but they have different numbers of neutrons. Most elements occur as two or more isotopes in nature. A mass spectrometer is used to separate atoms of slightly different masses, so it can separate the isotopes of samples of naturally occurring elements which are mixtures of isotopes.

The **atomic mass** (also known as **atomic weight**) of an element is the weighted average of the masses of the isotopes of that element. Therefore, if 92.0% of the atoms of an element have a mass of 28.0 amu, 6.0% have a mass of 29.0 amu, and the rest (2.0%) have a mass of 30.0 amu, the average atomic mass is (0.92)(28.0 amu) + (0.06)(29.0 amu) + (0.02)(30.0 amu) = 25.76 amu + 1.74 amu + 0.60 amu = 28.1 amu which makes it silicon. An **atomic mass unit (amu)** is defined as one-twelfth of the mass of a carbon atom that contains six protons and six neutrons.

As the masses of the elements were found, the elements were placed on a table to try to organize them. The **Periodic Table of the Elements** used today is based on the one created by Dmitri Mendeleev who saw that many of the elements were metals and that most of the elements could be grouped according to various properties. Each box in the table shows at least four pieces of data: (1) the element symbol represented by one or two letters, the first letter is capitalized with the second one being lower case, (2) the element name, (3) the atomic number, and (4) the atomic weight. The elements are arranged in the periodic table in vertical columns called groups or families which have similar chemical properties and in horizontal rows called periods which are based on their electron configurations. When Mendeleev's table appeared, there were blank spots where properties of an element were predicted but the element had not been discovered. Elements discovered after his table fit those blanks.

Electrons determine the chemical behavior of an element. Each electron in an atom can be described by a unique set of four quantum numbers, n, l, m and s. The principal quantum number (n = 1, 2, 3,…) is the number of the energy level (sometimes called the electron shell number) and describes the relative electron cloud size (how many electrons and what level and sublevel). The seven principal quantum numbers correspond to the seven periods (rows) on the periodic table. Each energy level has sublevels (s, p, d, and f) of the principal quantum number.

The second quantum number (l = 0, 1, 2, …which is $n - 1$) describes the shape of the cloud. The third quantum number, m, describes the orientation in space of each orbital. Each orbital may contain a maximum of one pair of electrons. Electrons in the same orbital have opposite spins. Accordingly, the fourth quantum number (s = + ½ or − ½) describes the spin direction of the electron. Pauli's exclusion principle states that no two electrons in an atom can have the same set of quantum numbers.

The s subshell has one orbital which can have up to two electrons, the p subshell which can have up to three orbitals with six electrons, the d subshell has five orbitals which can have up to ten electrons, and the f subshell has seven orbitals which can have up to fourteen electrons. Subshells fill in the order in which the arrows are shown:

$1s^2$			
$2s^2$	$2p^6$		
$3s^2$	$3p^6$	$3d^{10}$	
$4s^2$	$4p^6$	$4d^{10}$	$4f^{14}$
$5s^2$	$5p^6$	$5d^{10}$	$5f^{14}$
$6s^2$	$6p^6$	$6d^{10}$	
$7s^2$	$7p^6$		

For example: Hydrogen is $1s^1$ and Helium is $1s^2$. Oxygen has an atomic number of eight, so it has eight electrons or $1s^2\,2s^2\,2p^4$. Iodine with 53 electrons could be notated as $1s^2\ 2s^2\ 2p^6\ 3s^2\ 3p^6\ 4s^2\ 3d^{10}\ 4p^6\ 5s^2\ 4d^{10}\ 5p^5$ or as (Kr) $5s^2\ 4d^{10}\ 5p^5$ using the configuration of the closest previous noble gas. Since the electrons fill the orbitals with opposite spins, the total electron configuration for Fluorine would be:

$1s^2$	$2s^2$	$2p^5$
X	X	X X \

Spin directions, shown by the two crosses of the X, are sometimes shown by an "up" arrow and a "down" arrow (↑ ↓). Electrons with the lowest energy are in orbitals closest to the nucleus with each energy level out from the nucleus taking more energy to attain. Electrons normally occupy the set of orbitals that give the atom the lowest overall energy.

 Periodic Properties

Noble gases have the most stable outer electron configurations. They are the least reactive of the elements. These "inert" gases are Group 8A because they have eight electrons (s^2p^6) in their outermost energy level.

The elements of Period 1A all (except Hydrogen) have one electron in their outermost energy level so they have an s^1 configuration. Therefore, they have one **valence electron** and, when they give that electron up to become an ion, they have a charge of +1. Positive ions are called **cations**. In general, elements with three or fewer electrons in their outermost energy level (at left, in aqua) are considered to be metals and lose their electrons to become cations.

The elements of Period 7A all (except Helium) have seven electrons in their outermost energy level so they have s^2p^5 configuration. Therefore, they have seven valence electrons, so they desire to add an electron to become an ion. That makes them **anions** (negative ions) with a charge of -1. Generally, elements with five or more electrons in their outermost energy level (at right, in salmon) are considered nonmetals and are likely to gain electrons to become anions.

The B elements are transition elements and most have two electrons in their outermost energy level. Metalloids, those elements along the heavy stair-step line, show properties of both metals and nonmetals. The two series below the main periodic table are called Lanthanoids (upper) and Actinoids (lower).

KEY FACTS ABOUT THE ELEMENTS

Group	Name	Configuration	Charges	Properties
1A	Alkali metals	s^1	+1	Reactive, hard, shiny, conduct heat & electricity, malleable, ductile, ionic, solid
2A	Alkaline earth metals	s^2	+2	Reactive, hard, shiny, conduct heat & electricity, malleable, ductile, ionic, solid
3A	Aluminum group	s^2p^1	+3	
4A	Carbon group	s^2p^2	+4 or -4	Covalent
5A	N & P group	s^2p^3	-3	
6A	Chalcogens	s^2p^4	-2	
7A	Halogens	s^2p^5	-1	Reactive, ionic, gas
8A	Noble gases	s^2p^6	0	Nonreactive, gas

Periodic Properties:

1. **Atomic Radius (Size)** – the radius of the atom measured from the center of the nucleus to the outermost electron or, if it is a covalent atomic radius it is measured as half the distance between the nuclei of two atoms of the diatomic molecule

2. **Electron Affinity** – energy change accompanying the addition of an electron to an atom to make a negative ion (anion)

3. **Ionic Size** – the radius of an ion measured from the center of the nucleus to the outermost electron. Going left to right there is a gradual decrease through the positive ions as they lose electrons and therefore an energy level, but Group 5 is much bigger due to keeping the energy level and gaining an electron and then there is a slight decrease going through Group 7.

4. **Electronegativity** – tendency for an atom to attract electrons to itself in bonding

5. **Shielding Effect** – a decrease in attraction between an atom's nucleus and its outer electrons due to the electrons between the nucleus and the outer electrons

6. **Ionization Energy** – energy necessary to remove an electron from an atom to make an ion. Factors affecting ionization energy:
   a. Nuclear charge – the larger the nuclear charge, the greater the IE
   b. Shielding effect – the greater the shielding effect, the less the IE
   c. Radius – the greater the distance between the nucleus and the outer electrons of an atom, the less the IE
   d. Sublevel – an electron from a sublevel that is more than half-full requires additional energy to be removed

Summary of periodic trends on the Periodic Table*:
*Note: Memorize the ones in italics; everything else increases top→bottom, left→right

Group Trends (top to bottom):

Increases: atomic radius, nuclear charge, ionic size, shielding effect, atomic number (number of protons, number of electrons)
Decreases: ionization energy, electron affinity, electronegativity

Period Trends (left to right):

Increases: electronegativity, nuclear charge, ionization energy, electron affinity, atomic number (number of protons, number of electrons)
Decreases all the way across: atomic radius
Decreases through cations (positive) and again through anions: ionic size
Stays the same left to right: shielding effect

Chemical Bonding

The primary types of bonding between or among atoms are ionic and covalent. Other types of bonding are hydrogen, metallic, van der Waals, and macromolecular. Atoms are most stable with eight electrons in their outermost energy level, so atoms will either gain or lose electrons to attain that configuration (**octet rule**).

IONIC AND METALLIC BONDING

Ions are atoms or groups of atoms with a positive or negative charge. The chart "key facts about elements" shows the charges on elemental ions and the paragraphs prior to the chart explain those charges. The ionization energies for electrons of elements with fewer than four in their outermost energy level are quite low, so it is relatively easy to draw those electrons away to satisfy the octet rule. The charge of cations equals the number of electrons lost and positive since they now have more protons (positive) than electrons (negative).

The electron affinities for elements on the right side of the periodic table are quite low which allows them to attract atoms to satisfy the octet rule. The charge of anions equals the number of electrons gained and negative since they now have more electrons (negative) than protons (positive).

Positive ions (cations) electrostatically attract negative ions (anions) to create an ionic compound through ionic bonding. The total positive charge equals the total negative charge, giving the compound a charge of zero. Nearly all ionic compounds are crystalline solids at room temperature. The ions form a specific and predictable shape of crystal by their orderly arrangement. A coordination number indicates the number of ions of opposite charge that surround each ion in a crystal.

Bond angles, total number of electron pairs, number of shared pairs, and number of unshared pairs determine the shape of a crystal. There are five basic shapes: linear (3 atoms), trigonal planar (4 atoms), tetrahedral (5 atoms), trigonal bipyramidal (6 atoms), and octahedral (7 atoms). The basic shapes have no unshared pairs of electrons. When there is an unshared pair of electrons, the shape and bond angles remain about the same but there is a blank spot where there had been a shared pair of electrons.

Molecules with three atoms can be linear (no unshared pairs of electrons or three unshared pairs of electrons (a variation of trigonal bipyramidal), or bent which is a variation of trigonal planar (1 unshared pair) or tetrahedral (2 unshared pairs). With four atoms, the shape can be trigonal planar (0 unshared pairs), or trigonal pyramidal (1 unshared pair) which is a variation of tetrahedral or T-shaped planar (2 unshared pairs) which is a variation of trigonal bipyramidal. A molecule of five atoms can have the shape of tetrahedral (0 unshared pairs) or irregular tetrahedron (1 unshared pair, a variation of trigonal bipyramidal), or square planar (2 unshared pairs, a variation of octahedral). With six atoms, the possible shapes are trigonal bipyramidal (0 unshared pairs) or square pyramidal (1 unshared pair, a variation of octahedral). Octahedral is the main choice for seven atoms.

Sample Molecule	Number of Atoms	Electron Pair Geometry	Total Number of Electron Pairs	Number of Shared Pairs	Number of Unshared Pairs	Molecular Shape
BeF_2	3	sp	2	2	0	Linear
GaF_3	4	sp^2	3	3	0	Trigonal planar
O_3	3	sp^2	3	2	1	Bent
CH_4	5	sp^3	4	4	0	Tetrahedral
NH_3	4	sp^3	4	3	1	Trigonal pyramidal
H_2O	3	sp^3	4	2	2	Bent
$NbBr_5$	6	sp^3d	5	5	0	Trigonal bipyramidal
SF_4	5	sp^3d	5	4	1	Irregular tetrahedron
BrF_3	4	sp^3d	5	3	2	T-shaped Planar
XeF_2	3	sp^3d	5	2	3	Linear
SF_6	7	sp^3d^2	6	6	0	Octahedral
IF_5	6	sp^3d^2	6	5	1	Square pyramid
XeF_4	5	sp^3d^2	6	4	2	Square planar

Polyatomic ions are groups of atoms that behave as a unit and carry a charge just as an ion does and they combine with ions to form ionic compounds. Use the chart below to memorize the "-ate" ions; then remember (1) that "per-ate" means one more oxygen than "ate" but the same charge, (2) that "-ite" means one less oxygen than "-ate" but the same charge, and (3) that "hypo-ite" means one less oxygen than "-ite" but the same charge.

POLYATOMIC IONS AND THEIR CHARGES

Charge	Ions	Names
-3	PO_4	Phosphate
-2	O_2 SO_4 CO_3 CrO_4 Cr_2O_7	Peroxide Sulfate Carbonate Chromate Dichromate
-1	OH ClO_3 MnO_4 CN	Hydroxide Chlorate Permanganate Cyanide
+1	H NH_4 Metal(I)	Hydrogen Ammonium All metals with a Roman numeral I (-ous)
+2	Metal(II)	All metals with a Roman numeral II
+3	Metal(III)	All metals with a Roman numeral III
+4	Metal(IV)	All metals with a Roman numeral IV
+5	Metal(V)	All metals with a Roman numeral V

Metals are like ionic compounds in some ways. They consist of positive metal ions packed together and surrounded by a sea of their valence electrons to create the metallic bond. The valence electrons are free to travel from one end of a piece of metal to the other, accounting for the excellent electrical conductivity, malleability, and ductility. Metals are simple crystalline solids, usually in one of three basic shapes – body-centered cubic, face-centered cubic, or hexagonal close-packed arrangement.

COVALENT BONDING

Covalent Bonding is the sharing of electrons to acquire a stable electron configuration to create a **molecular compound**. A shared pair of electrons forms a **single covalent bond**. If two or three pairs of electrons are shared, double or triple bonds are formed. When only one of the atoms in a bond provides the pair of bonding electrons, it is a **coordinate covalent bond.** Molecular compounds tend to have relatively low melting and boiling points and often exist as gases or liquids at room temperature and may be composed of two or more nonmetallic elements (example: CO_2). Organic compounds are covalently bonded (see section on organic chemistry).

If the bonding electrons are shared equally, the bond is nonpolar. However, if the bonding electrons are shared unequally, the bond is polar and the amount of polarity is determined by consulting a table of electronegativities. If the electronegativity difference is less than 0.4 the bond is nonpolar covalent, if it is a 0.4 to 1.0 difference the bond is moderately polar covalent, and if it is 1.0-2 the bond is very polar covalent. (An electronegativity difference greater than 2.0 indicates an ionic bond.) In a **polar molecule,** one end has negative character and the other end has positive character, creating a dipole. The shape of the molecule as well as the polarity of each bond affects the polarity of the whole molecule.

Just as there are atomic orbitals (*s, p, d, f*), there are **molecular orbitals** produced when two atoms combine and their orbitals overlap. The overlap of two atomic orbitals produces two molecular orbitals, one of which is a bonding orbital and the other is an antibonding orbital. The bonding orbital has a lower energy than the atomic orbitals from which it is formed and the antibonding orbital has a higher energy than that of either of the atomic orbitals from which it is formed.

INTERMOLECULAR ATTRACTIONS

A great variety of physical properties occurs among covalent compounds due to **intermolecular attractions**, those attractions that occur *between molecules*. They are responsible for whether the molecular compound is a gas, a liquid, or a solid. They are weaker than either ionic or covalent bonding though. The weakest forces are called **van der Waals forces** and include dispersion forces and dipole interactions. **Dispersion forces** are caused by the motion of electrons. Molecules with few electrons such as fluorine tend to be gases due to weak dispersion force attraction, while molecules with more electrons like bromine tend to be liquids and those with even more attraction due to more electrons tend to be solids at room temperature. **Dipole interactions** are a type of electrostatic attraction between polar molecules. Because the hydrogens in water have a slightly positive charge and the oxygen has a slightly negative charge, the hydrogens in one molecule are attracted to oxygens in other molecules. This attraction pulls the molecules closer together and contributes to the spherical drop of water.

A **hydrogen bond** is a weak, secondary bond between a partially positive hydrogen atom and a partially negative (highly electronegative) N, O, or F atom in the same molecule or a nearby molecule. Hydrogen bonds are the strongest of the intermolecular forces. The properties of water and biological molecules like proteins are greatly determined by hydrogen bonds.

Network solids are substances in which all the atoms are covalently bonded to each other. Diamond, made entirely of carbon, is a network solid because each carbon is covalently bonded to four other carbons. Network solids have very high melting points.

Compounds

A compound is a pure substance formed from the combination of two or more elements that differs from the elements in it. Compounds obey the **law of definite proportions** which says that the elements in a compound always combine in the same proportion by mass. All compounds are electrically neutral. There are two types of compounds: **ionic compounds** are formed using ions and use electrostatic charge and attraction while **molecular compounds** are formed of covalently bonded atoms. The smallest unit of either one is sometimes referred to as a **molecule**; however, the molecule is the smallest unit of a molecular compound while a **formula unit** is the smallest unit of an ionic compound.

SUMMARY OF CHARACTERISTICS OF IONIC AND COVALENT COMPOUNDS

Characteristic	Ionic Compound	Covalent Compound
Representative unit	Formula unit	Molecule
Bond Formation	Transfer of one or more electrons between atoms	Sharing of electron pairs between atoms
Physical State	Solid	Solid, Liquid, or Gas
Type of Elements	Metallic and nonmetallic	Nonmetallic
Melting Point	High	Low
Solubility in Water	High	High to Low
Electrical conductivity	Good	Poor

The composition of each compound is represented by a **chemical formula** which shows the kinds and numbers of atoms in a formula unit of an ionic compound or a **molecular formula** which shows the number and kinds of atoms present in a molecule of a molecular compound. The **law of multiple proportions** states that whenever two elements form more than one compound, the different masses of one element that combine with the same mass of the other element are in the ratio of small whole numbers.

Naming Compounds

<u>Naming Binary Ionic Compounds in which the cation has only one valence</u> (such as 1A, 2A, and aluminum):

1. The cation is named first, the anion second.
2. A monatomic cation takes its name from the name of the element.
3. A monatomic anion is named by taking the first part of the element name and adding –ide.
4. Examples: sodium chloride is NaCl, lithium nitride is Li_3N

<u>Naming Binary Ionic Compounds in which the cation has more than one valence</u> (such as transition ions):

1. The charge on the metal ion must be specified, such as iron(II) and iron(III) denoting Fe^{+2} and Fe^{+3} respectively. In an older method, the ion with the lower charge has a name ending in –ous (Ferrous = Fe^{+2}) and the ion with the higher charge has a name ending in –ic (Ferric = Fe^{+3}).
2. The cation is named first, the anion second.
3. A monatomic anion is named by taking the first part of the element name and adding –ide.
4. Examples: iron(III) oxide (ferric oxide) is Fe_2O_3, tin(IV) chloride is $SnCl_4$

<u>Naming Binary Covalent Compounds</u> (between two nonmetals):

1. The first element in the formula is named first using the full element name.
2. The second element is named as if it were an anion.
3. Prefixes are used to denote the numbers of atoms present. These prefixes are *di-* for two, *tri-* for three, *tetra-* for four, *penta-* for five, etc. No prefix is needed for a single atom which is the first element named.
4. Examples: silicon tetrabromide is $SiBr_4$, dinitrogen monoxide is N_2O

<u>Naming Acids:</u>

1. Normally, the cation in acids is H^+ and the compounds are dissolved in water or give water as a product. Most of these compounds can be named two ways.
2. When the anion ends in –ide, the acid name begins with the prefix *hydro-* such that HCl is hydrogen chloride or hydrochloric acid and H_2S is hydrogen sulfide or hydrosulfuric acid.
3. Polyatomic ions ending in –ate become –ic acids such that $HClO_3$ is hydrogen chlorate or chloric acid and $HClO_4$ is hydrogen perchlorate or perchloric acid.
4. Polyatomic ions ending in –ite become –ous acids such that $HClO_2$ is hydrogen chlorite or chlorous acid and HClO is hydrogen hypochlorite or hypochlorous acid.

The Mole Concept

The term representative particle refers to the smallest unit of a substance which can be an atom, an ion, or a molecule. Normally the representative particle of an element is an atom. Seven elements do not exist as single atoms in nature, but as diatomic molecules. They are easy to remember using a rule of 7's: there are seven of them, they make a 7 on the Periodic Table, and most are in Period 7A – nitrogen (N_2), oxygen (O_2), fluorine (F_2), chlorine (Cl_2), bromine (Br_2), iodine (I_2) plus hydrogen (H_2).

In 1809, Joseph Gay-Lussac found that two volumes of hydrogen reacted with one volume of oxygen (at the same temperature and pressure) to form two volumes of water and that one volume of hydrogen reacted with one volume of chlorine to form two volumes of hydrogen chloride. In 1811, Amedeo Avogadro's hypothesis interpreted Joseph Gay-Lussac's work: Equal volumes of different gases at the same temperature and pressure contain the same number of particles. Under these conditions the volume of a gas is determined by the number of molecules present. Thus,

$$2\ H_2 + O_2 \rightarrow 2\ H_2O \quad \text{and} \quad 2\ H_2 + Cl_2 \rightarrow 2\ HCl$$

The number of particles in one "volume" of hydrogen is the same as the number of particles in one "volume" of any other element just as the number of eggs in a dozen is always twelve. That number of particles, the **mole**, is named **Avogadro's number** and is equal to 6.02 x 1023. For example, one mole of magnesium is 6.02 x 1023 atoms of magnesium and one mole of oxygen is 6.02 x 1023 molecules, but since each molecule has two atoms it is (2 atoms/molecule)(6.02 x 1023 molecules) or 1.204 x 1024 atoms. Notice that in (atoms/~~molecule~~)(~~molecule~~) the molecules cancel each other.

The **gram atomic mass** is the number of grams of an element that is numerically equal to the atomic mass in amu. For hydrogen, the gram atomic mass is 1 amu just as the gram atomic mass of carbon is 12 amu (its atomic weight). The mass of one mole of a compound is its **gram formula mass** which is the total of the gram atomic masses multiplied by their subscripts in the formula of the elements.

Example: *Calculate the gram formula mass of Al2(SO4)3 aluminum sulfate*:

The subscript of 2 next to Al means there are two moles of aluminum, so aluminum's atomic mass must be multiplied by two.

The subscript of 4 with the O means there are four moles of oxygen in sulfate, so the atomic mass of oxygen must be multiplied by four.

The subscript of 3 with the SO_4 means there are three moles of sulfate. In this case, sulfur's atomic mass must be multiplied by three and oxygen's must be multiplied by 3 x 4 (above) or 12.

For Al: 2 moles x 28.98 g/mole = 57.96 g
For O: 12 moles x 16.00 g/mole = 152.00 g
For S: 3 moles x 32.06 g/mole = 96.18 g
Total of Gram Formula Mass = 57.96 g + 152.00 g + 96.18 g = 306.14 g

The term **molar mass** can be used in place of gram formula mass to refer to the mass of a mole of atoms or molecules or formula units of any element or compound.

Conversions between moles and grams of a substance are done using the gram formula mass such that moles of substance x gram formula mass = grams of substance. Using this formula, moles x grams/mole allows moles to cancel and leaves you with grams. If the number of grams is known, flip the gram formula mass upside down (1 mole of carbon = 12 grams or 12 grams of carbon = 1 mole can be expressed and used as 1 mole C / 12 g C or 12 g C / 1 mole C) and multiply by the mass to cancel grams and get moles.

Example 1: *Find the mass in grams of 5.0 mol H_2O_2.* The gram formula mass of H_2O_2 is 2(1 g H/mol H) + 2(16 g O/mol O) = 2 g + 32 g = 34 g/mol H_2O_2.
5.0 mol H_2O_2 x 34 g H_2O_2 / 1 mol H_2O_2 = 170 grams H_2O_2

Example 2: *Find the number of moles in 333 g SnF_2.* The gram formula mass of SnF_2 is 1(118.69 g Sn/mol Sn) + 2(18.00 g F_2/mol F_2) = 118.69 g + 36 g = 154.69 g/mol SnF_2.
333 g SnF_2 x 1 mol SnF_2 / 154.69 g SnF_2 = 2.15 mol SnF_2

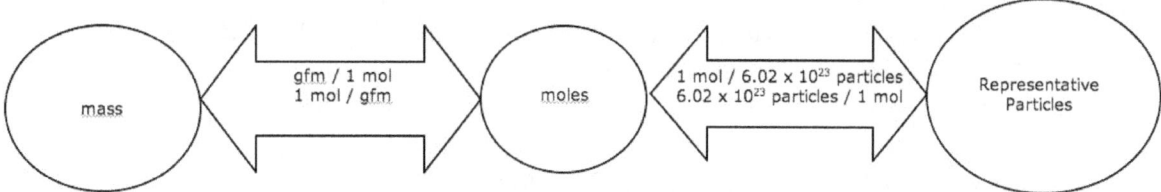

Percent Composition and Empirical Formula

Percent composition is the percent by mass of each element in a compound. It includes as many percents as there are elements in the compound.

Example: *Calculate the percent composition of the compound formed from 222.6 g of Na and 77.4 g of O.* Add the two masses to find the total mass of the compound:
222.6 + 77.4 g = 300.0 g
% element = mass element / mass of compound x 100 %
% Na = mass Na / mass of cmpd x 100 % = 222.6 g Na / 300.0 g Na_xO_x = 74.2 % Na
% O = 77.4 g O / 300 g a_xO_x x 100 % = 25.8 % O
The two percentages have to add up to 100%: 74.2% + 25.8% = 100%

To calculate the percent by mass of an element in a known compound, divide the mass of the element in one mole by the gram formula mass of the compound and multiply by 100%.

Percent composition can be used to calculate the number of grams of an element in a specific amount of a compound.

Example: *Using the percent composition, calculate the amount of hydrogen in 378 g HCN.* Use the subscripts as the number of moles, so H = 1, C = 1, and N = 1.
(1 mol H) (1 g H / 1 mol H) = 1 g H
(1 mol C) (12 g C / 1 mol C) = 12 g C
(1 mol N) (14 g N / 1 mol N) = 14 g N
Gram formula mass (gfm) of HCN = 1 g + 12 g + 14 g = 27 g HCN
% H = 1 g H / 27 g HCN x 100% = 3.7 % H
% C = 12 g C / 27 g HCN x 100% = 44.4 % C
% N = 14 g N / 27 g HCN x 100% = 51.9 % N
Check: 3.7 % + 44.4 % + 51.9 % = 100.0 %
grams H = (3.7 %)(1 / 100%)(378 g H) = 14.0 g H

An **empirical formula** is the formula with the lowest whole-number ratio of elements in a compound such that the empirical formula for hydrogen peroxide (H_2O_2) is HO.

Example: *Calculate the empirical formula of a compound that is 79.8% C and 20.2% H.*

Assume 100 grams of the compound. Therefore, 79.8 g are C and 20.2 g are H. Use gram formula mass to convert to moles. (79.8 g C)(1 mol C / 12 g C) = 6.65 mol C and

(20.2 g H)(1 mol H / 1 g H) = 20.2 mol H. This does not give a whole number ratio – 6.65:20.2 so divide 20.2 by 6.65 to get 3.04 which is pretty close to the whole number 3. That means that there are 3 H for every C, so the empirical formula is CH_3.

The molecular formula of a compound can be determined from its empirical formula and its gram formula mass. Once the empirical formula is found, calculate its mass. Then divide the known gram formula mass by the empirical mass to find what number to use to multiply all the subscripts of the empirical formula.

Example: *Determine the molecular formula for a compound that is 94.1 % O and 5.9 % H and has a gram formula mass of 34 grams.*
(0.941 g̶ O̶)(1 mol O / 16 g̶ O̶) = 0.059 mol O
(0.059 g̶ H̶)(1 mol H / 1 g̶ H̶) = 0.059 mol H
Since this is a 1:1 ratio, the empirical formula is HO.
The empirical mass = 1 g H + 16 g O = 17 g HO.
The gram formula mass is 34 grams; therefore, 34 grams / 17 grams = 2.
Multiply the subscripts (of 1) by 2 to get a molecular formula of H_2O_2

Gases

The **Kinetic Theory** says that the tiny particles in all forms of matter are in constant motion. These particles may be atoms, ions, or molecules in gases, liquids, or solids. The basic assumptions of the kinetic theory of gases are that (1) a gas is composed of tiny particles (molecules or atoms) of negligible size with distance between them, (2) the particles in a gas move rapidly in constant random motion and collide with each other, and (3) all the collisions are perfectly elastic. The behavior of gases depends on their volume, temperature, and pressure.

The energy an object has because of its motion is called kinetic energy. The average kinetic energy of the particles of a substance is proportional to the temperature of the substance. As the temperature rises, the particles move faster due to increased thermal energy. This causes an increased number of collisions. The collisions produce a measurable force known as pressure.

The volume of a gas is usually measured at **STP, standard temperature (0° Celsius or 273° Kelvin) and pressure (1 atmosphere).** At STP one mole of any gas occupies a volume of **22.4 liters**, a quantity known as the **molar volume** of the given gas.

Example 1: *What is the volume at STP of 3.20×10^{-2} mol CO_2?*
(3.20×10^{-2} m̶o̶l̶ C̶O̶$_2$)(22.4 L CO_2 / 1 m̶o̶l̶ C̶O̶$_2$) = 0.717 L CO_2

<u>Example 2</u>: *Assuming STP, how many moles are in 5.42×10^{-1} mL Ne?*
$(5.42 \times 10^{-1} \text{ mL Ne})(1 \text{ L} / 1000 \text{ mL})(1 \text{ mol Ne} / 22.4 \text{ L Ne}) = 2.42 \times 10^{-5}$ mol Ne

The **density of a gas** is usually measured in grams per liter. The experimentally determined density of a gas at STP is used to calculate the gram formula mass of that gas which can be an element or a compound.

<u>Example</u>: *The density of a gas is 2.86 g/L at STP. Determine the gram formula mass of the compound. Is it ammonia (NH_4), sulfur dioxide (SO_2), or methane (CH_4)?*
$(22.4 \text{ L}/1 \text{ mol})(2.86 \text{ g/L}) = 64.1$ g/mol
$NH_4 = (1)(14 \text{ g/mol}) + (4)(1 \text{ g/mol}) = 14 \text{ g/mol} + 4 \text{ g/mol} = 18$ g/mol
$SO_2 = (1)(32 \text{ g/mol}) + (2)(16 \text{ g/mol}) = 32 \text{ g/mol} + 32 \text{ g/mol} = 64$ g/mol
$CH_4 = (1)(12 \text{ g/mol}) + (4)(1 \text{ g/mol}) = 12 \text{ g/mol} + 4 \text{ g/mol} = 16$ g/mol
Therefore, the compound is SO_2.

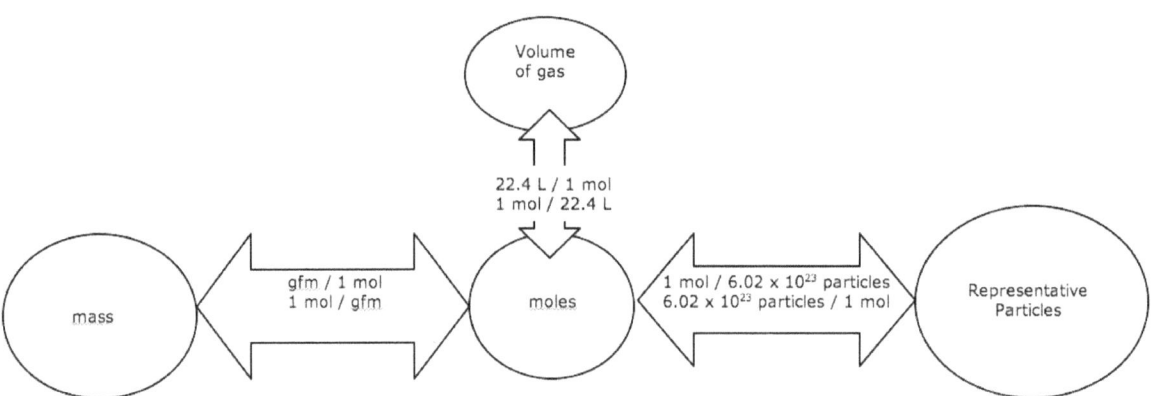

Gas Laws

The gas laws are a set of equations that apply equally to all gases and show relationships among pressure, volume, temperature, moles, and number of particles. A few conversions and constants need to be remembered:
1 atmosphere (atm) = 760 mm Hg
Kelvin (K) = °C + 273
Ideal gas constant (R) = 0.082 L-atm/K-mol

Dalton's Law of Partial Pressures: Gases in a single container all have the same volume and are at the same temperature, so the difference in their partial pressures is due only to the difference in the numbers of molecules present. $P_{total} = P_1 + P_2 + P_3 \ldots$

Boyle's Law: At a constant temperature, the pressure of a gas will vary inversely with the volume. In other words, if a given volume of gas has more pressure exerted upon it, it will take less volume. $P_1V_1 = P_2V_2$

Charles' Law: At a constant pressure, the volume of a given amount of gas will vary proportionately with the temperature expressed in Kelvin. Expressed differently, increasing the temperature of a given volume of gas will cause the molecules to move faster and take up more volume. $V_1T_2 = V_2T_1$

Avogadro's Law: Equal volumes of all gases contain the same number of molecules such that **V/n = constant (22.4 liters/mole).**

Boyle's Law and Charles' Law become the **Combined Gas Law**: $P_1V_1T_2 = P_2V_2T_1$. The **Ideal Gas Equation** combines this and Avogadro's Law as **PV = nRT** where n is the number of particles and R is a constant called the ideal gas constant whose value depends on the units used.

Example 1: *The pressure in an automobile tire is 2.0 atm at 27°C. At the end of a journey on a hot sunny day, the pressure has risen to 2.2 atm. Assuming the volume has not changed, what is the temperature of the air in the tire?* Use the combined gas law, but drop out volume:
$P_1V_1T_2 = P_2V_2T_1$ so it becomes $P_1T_2 = P_2T_1$ or $T_2 = P_2T_1 / P_1$
T_2 = (2.2 atm)(27°C + 273 K) / 2.0 atm = 330.0 K or (330-273) = 57°C

Example 2: *What volume will 12.0 g of oxygen gas occupy at 25°C and a pressure of 0.520 atm?*
PV = nRT   (0.520 atm)(V) = (12.0 g O_2)(1 mole O_2/32 g O_2)(0.0821 L-atm/K-mol)(25 + 273 K)
V = 17.6 L O_2

The particles of ideal gases have no volume and no attraction, but real gases have both volume and mutual attraction. At high pressures and low temperatures, these two factors affect the behavior of gases. At normal laboratory conditions most common gases act like ideal gases. The lower the critical temperature of a gas, the more nearly it behaves as an ideal gas.

Liquids and Solids

Since the particles of both **liquids** and gases are in constant motion and are free to slide past each other, they can flow and are referred to as fluids. However, the particles of liquids are held together by weak attractive forces which must be overcome for those particles to escape the liquid. These forces also reduce the space between particles. Vapor pressure, heat of vaporization, and boiling point of a liquid are determined by the interplay of the motion of the particles, heat, and pressure.

Vaporization is the conversion of a liquid to a gas (or vapor). It is the escape of molecules from the surface of the liquid. Only those molecules which possess enough kinetic energy can escape the bonds at the surface. Some that escape collide with air molecules and fall back into the liquid, called **condensation**. The liquid **evaporates** (becomes vapor) faster when heated.

Vapor pressure is created in an enclosed container which is heated to vaporize a liquid. The vapor molecules cannot escape the container, so some remain in the space above the liquid and some go back into the liquid. When the volume of those evaporating equals the volume of those condensing, a **dynamic equilibrium** is reached so that the rate of evaporation equals the rate of condensation.

Boiling point is the temperature at which the vapor pressure of the liquid is just equal to the external pressure. The boiling point of a liquid at a pressure of 1 atm is the normal boiling point of that liquid. At higher external pressures, a liquid's boiling point increases. The temperature of a boiling liquid never rises above its boiling point.

The particles in **solids** are tightly packed against each other, so that instead of random movements the particles in solids vibrate and rotate about fixed points. Solids are dense and incompressible and do not flow.

Most solids are crystalline. In **crystals** the atoms, ions, or molecules are arranged in an orderly, repeating, three-dimensional pattern called the crystal lattice. Each substance has a specific characteristic crystal lattice shape that does not vary. There are seven crystal systems that differ based on the angles between the faces and how many of the edges of the faces are equal. The seven crystal shapes are cubic, tetragonal, orthorhombic, monoclinic, triclinic, hexagonal, and rhombohedral.

The unit cell is the smallest group of particles within a crystal that retains the geometric shape of the crystal. Each crystal system has one to four types of unit cells. For example, there are three unit cells that are part of the cubic crystal system: cubic, face-centered cubic, and body-centered cubic. The melting points of crystals are determined by how the atoms are bonded.

When a solid is heated, its particles vibrate faster and the kinetic energy increases. The **melting point** is the temperature at which the solid turns into a liquid because the vibrations of some of the particles are strong enough to overcome the interactions that hold them in fixed positions. The melting point is the same as the freezing point.

Some substances such as carbon can exist in more than one type of solid state. Under tremendous pressure it crystallizes into diamond (compact symmetrical), but under less pressure it crystallizes into graphite (sheets with weak bonds). Soot is also carbon, but with the atoms randomly bonded to one another.

Some solids are **amorphous** and lack an ordered internal structure. Examples are rubber, plastic, and asphalt. Another amorphous solid is glass which does not melt at a specific temperature but gradually soften when heated.

Sublimation is the phase change from solid to vapor without going through liquid. A good example is dry ice, CO_2.

Phase Changes

A phase change occurs when the physical state of a substance changes such as a solid melting to liquid or a gas condensing to liquid.

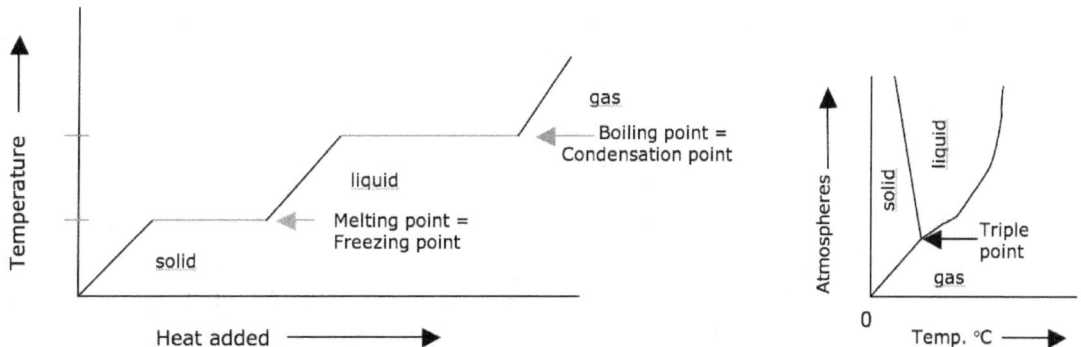

When a phase change occurs the temperature of the substance remains constant. As heat is absorbed the energy causes a change of state instead of a change of temperature. The **heat of fusion** is the heat required to melt one gram of a solid at its melting point. The heat of fusion of water is 80 cal/g, the energy to change 1 g of ice to 1 g water at 0°C. The heat of fusion equals the **heat of solidification**, the amount of heat given up as one gram of liquid changes to a solid at the melting point. The heat of vaporization is the heat required to change 1 g of a liquid to gas at the boiling point of that liquid. For water, the **heat of vaporization** is 540 cal/g. The **heat of condensation** equals the heat of vaporization. It is the heat released when 1 g of a gas condenses to a liquid at the boiling point. The **triple point** is the temperature and pressure at which solid, liquid and gas are in equilibrium.

Example: *Calculate the energy required to change 40 g of ice at -27°C to steam at 150°C.*

Heat 40 g of ice from -27°C to 0°C: (40 g)(1 cal/g°C)(27°C) = 1,080 cal = 1.08 kcal
Phase change 40 g ice to water at 0°C: (40 g)(80 cal/g) = 3,200 cal = 3.20 kcal
Heat 40 g of water from 0°C to 100°C: (40 g)(1 cal/g°C)(100°C) = 4,000 cal = 4.00 kcal
Phase change 40 g water to 40 g steam at 100°C: (40 g)(540 cal/g) = 21,600 cal = 21.60 kcal
Heat 40 g steam to 150°C: (40 g)(1 cal/g°C)(50°C) = 2,000 cal = 2.00 kcal
40 g of ice at -27°C to steam at 150°C: 1.08 kcal + 3.20 kcal + 4.00 kcal + 21.6 kcal + 2.00 kcal = 31.88 kcal of energy

Solutions

Aqueous solutions are water samples containing dissolved substances. The dissolving medium (water) is called the **solvent** and the dissolved particles of a substance are called the **solute**. The **rate of solubility** can be increased by (1) increasing the temperature, (2) agitating by stirring or shaking the solution, or (3) decreasing the solute particle size to create more surface area.

Water molecules are dipoles, so molecules which are dipoles dissolve well in it. With all the molecules in constant motion, it is easy for the H^+ end of H_2O to attract the negative ions and the O^{-2} end of H_2O to attract the positive ions, thus breaking the bonds between positive and negative ions of the solute. **Solvation** occurs when those ions are surrounded by water molecules. Sometimes ionic compounds have stronger attractive forces than the attractive forces exerted by water. Those compounds, like barium sulfate and calcium carbonate, are insoluble ionic compounds.

Nonpolar molecules do not dissolve much in water, but must be dissolved in a nonpolar solvent such as benzene. As a rule, "like dissolves like" holds true since polar solvents like water dissolve polar and ionic compounds and nonpolar solvents dissolve nonpolar and organic compounds.

Solid, liquid, and gaseous solutions exist. Metal alloys are solid solutions and air is a gaseous solution. Liquids that are soluble in one another are **miscible**. Polar liquids are usually miscible with water, but nonpolar liquids tend to be immiscible with water. The solubilities of gases are greater in cold water than in hot water as the dissolved gases tend to escape the water as vapor. **Henry's Law** applies to gases in liquids: at a given temperature the solubility of a gas in a liquid (S) is directly proportional to the pressure of the gas above the liquid (P) such that $S_1P_2 = S_2P_1$.

The **solubility** of a substance is the amount of substance that dissolves in a given quantity of a given solvent at a given temperature to produce a saturated solution. A **saturated solution** contains the maximum amount of solute for a given amount of solvent at a constant temperature and pressure. In a saturated solution the dissolved and undissolved solute are in dynamic equilibrium. Some solutions can be **supersaturated** under special conditions, allowing more solute than the solvent can theoretically hold to be dissolved. An **unsaturated solution** is one that contains less than the maximum amount of solute for that amount of that solvent at that temperature and pressure.

Concentrations – Molarity, Molality, and Normality

The **concentration** of a solution is a measure of the amount of solute that is dissolved in a standard quantity of solvent. The terms dilute (small amount of solute) and concentrated (large of amount of solute) are qualitative and not quantitative and therefore, not useful in chemistry.

The most important unit of concentration is **molarity** (M) which is the number of moles of a solute dissolved in 1 liter of solution (not solvent, but total solution).

$$\text{Molarity } (M) = \frac{\text{number of moles of solute}}{\text{number of liters of solution}}$$

Example: *A saline solution contains 0.90 g of NaCl per 100 mL of solution. What is its molarity?* Remember the gram formula mass of NaCl is 58.5 g/mol
$M = (0.90 \text{ g})(1\text{mol}/58.5 \text{ g}) / (100 \text{ mL})(1 \text{ L}/1000 \text{ mL}) = 0.15 \, M$ solution

The number of moles of solute does not change when a solution is diluted. Changing the quantity of solvent does not change the quantity of solute. Therefore, $\mathbf{M_1 V_1 = M_2 V_2}$.

Another method of expressing concentration is **percent** which can be volume/volume or mass/volume percent. Percent by volume means **volume of solute divided by volume of total solution, then multiplied by 100%.**

Equivalents are used to express concentration for acid-base neutralizations. The mass of one equivalent of a substance is called its gram equivalent mass. One **equivalent** is the amount of an acid (or base) that will give one mole of hydrogen (or hydroxide) ions. One mole of HBr is one equivalent of HBr, so its **gram equivalent mass** is 90 grams. However, one mole of H_2SO_4 is two equivalents (has two hydrogens), so its gram formula mass of 98 grams is double its gram equivalent mass of 49 grams. **Normality** (N) of a solution is the **number of equivalents of solute in 1 L of solution**, or **molarity** times the number of ionizable hydrogens. Dilutions can be made using the formula: $N_1V_1 = N_2V_2$.

A fourth method of expressing concentration is **molality** (m) which is **moles of solute per kilogram (1000 g) of solvent**.

 Colligative Properties

The boiling point of a solution is higher than the boiling point of the pure solvent. Adding a solute to the solvent decreases the solvent's vapor pressure, so additional kinetic energy must be added to raise the vapor pressure of the liquid phase to atmospheric pressure. The boiling point of water increases by 0.52°C for every mole of particles that the solute forms when dissolved in 1000 g of water. Since the boiling point of water is dependent on the number of particles dissolved in a given mass of solvent, it is a **colligative property**. The amount of **boiling point elevation** is directly proportional to the molal concentration such that

$\Delta T_b = K_b m$

The proportionality constant K_b is in the units °C/molal and is specific to the solvent. Once the ΔT_b has been calculated, it must be added to the normal boiling point of that solvent to get the new boiling point. The K_b for water is 0.512 °C/m.

Adding a solute to a solvent disrupts the pattern of the crystal lattice. More kinetic energy must be withdrawn from the solution than from the pure solvent for solidification to occur. The difference in temperature between the freezing point of the solvent and the freezing point of the solution is the **freezing point depression**. This is a colligative property since it is dependent on the number of particles of solute. This amount is calculated like the boiling point elevation, but a K_f for the solvent is used and the ΔT_f is subtracted from the normal freezing point of the solvent.

$\Delta T_f = K_f m$ $\quad$ K_f for water is 1.86 °C/m

Raoult's Law uses mole fraction as a measure of concentration when colligative properties like vapor pressure are concerned. **Mole fraction** is **number of moles of solvent divided by the combined numbers of moles of solvent and solute**. Raoult's Law says that **vapor pressure of the solution is equal to mole fraction of the solvent times the vapor pressure of the solvent**.

Acids and Bases

Historically there are three definitions of acids and bases:

	Arrhenius	Bronsted-Lowry	Lewis
Acid definition	H+	H+ donor	Electron pair acceptor
Base definition	OH-	H+ acceptor	Electron pair donor

In the broadest definition, the Lewis definition, the acid is seen as becoming more negative and the base is seen as becoming more positive.

Arrhenius said all acids must start with H+ and all bases must end with OH-. He believed that an acid like HCl had one proton or H+ to donate so it was monoprotic. In the same way, H_2SO_4 had two so it was diprotic and H_2PO_4 had three so it was triprotic. Acids did not have to have bases to go with them and bases did not necessarily have acids with them.

The Bronsted-Lowry definition looked at an equation rather than a formula. Acid-base equations had conjugate acid-base pairs:

```
            ┌─── conjugate acid base pair ───┐
            ▼                                ▼
   NH₃    +    H₂O    ⇌    NH₄⁺    +    OH⁻
Can accept H⁺  Can donate H⁺  Can donate H⁺  Can accept H⁺
   Base        Acid           Acid           Base
            ▲                                ▲
            └─── conjugate acid base pair ───┘
```

NH_3 + H_2O ⇌ NH_4^+ + OH^-

- NH_3: Can accept H⁺, Base
- H_2O: Can donate H⁺, Acid
- NH_4^+: Can donate H⁺, Acid
- OH^-: Can accept H⁺, Base

The Lewis dot structures are useful to Lewis' definition. In the equation

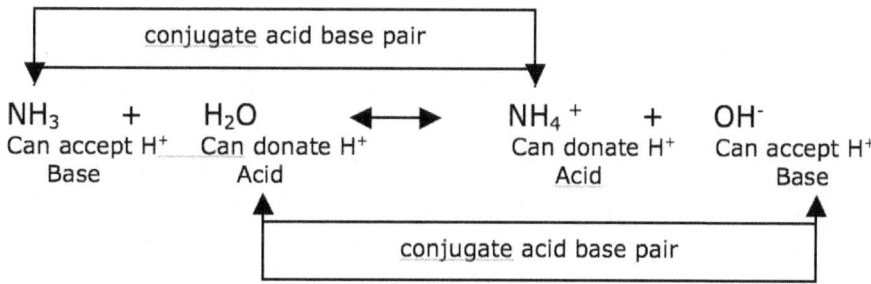

Ammonia is donating a pair of electrons, making it a Lewis base. Boron trifluoride is accepting a pair of electrons, making it a Lewis acid.

Aqueous solutions of acids conduct electricity, so are electrolytes. Aqueous solutions of bases are also electrolytes. Many metals like magnesium react with aqueous solutions of acids to produce hydrogen gas. <u>Acids react with bases to form water and a salt.</u>

Amphoteric means that a substance can be an acid or a base depending on its circumstances. For example, water can donate a H+ which makes it an acid or it can accept a H+ which makes it a base. A water molecule that loses a hydrogen ion becomes a negatively charged hydroxide ion (OH^-). A water molecule that gains a hydrogen ion becomes a positively charged hydronium ion (H_3O^+). The reaction in which two water molecules react to give ions is the self-ionization of water: $H_2O \leftrightarrow H^+ + OH^-$. In pure water (a neutral solution) the concentration of hydrogen ions, $[H^+]$, and the concentration of hydroxide ions, $[OH^-]$, are equal at only 1.0×10^{-7} mol/L each. If $[H^+]$ increases, then $[OH^-]$ decreases. If additional ions of either type are added to the solution, the equilibrium shifts away from the ion side of the equation.

pH and pOH

The product of the concentrations of the hydrogen ions and the hydroxide ions in water is K_w, the ion-product constant for water: $[H^+] \times [OH^-] = 1.0 \times 10^{-14}$ mol/L $= K_w$

The pH scale is the method for expressing the hydrogen ion concentration and the pOH scale is the method for expressing the hydroxide ion concentration.

pH	0	1	2	3	4	5	6	7	8	9	10	11	12	13	14
$[H^+]$	10^0	10^{-1}	10^{-2}	10^{-3}	10^{-4}	10^{-5}	10^{-6}	10^{-7}	10^{-8}	10^{-9}	10^{-10}	10^{-11}	10^{-12}	10^{-13}	10^{-14}
	Acid							neutral							Base
$[OH^-]$	10^{-14}	10^{-13}	10^{-12}	10^{-11}	10^{-10}	10^{-9}	10^{-8}	10^{-7}	10^{-6}	10^{-5}	10^{-4}	10^{-3}	10^{-2}	10^{-1}	10^0
pOH	14	13	12	11	10	9	8	7	6	5	4	3	2	1	0

pH = - log $[H^+]$ and   pOH = - log $[OH^-]$
pH = - log (1×10^{-4}) and   pOH = - log (1×10^{-10})
pH = 4   and   pOH = 10   The pH + pOH must = 14

A pH below 7 is acid and corresponds to a pOH above 7. A pOH below 7 is basic and corresponds to a pH above 7.

Precipitates

Predicting the identity of a precipitate, a solid product in a reaction, requires knowledge of the solubilities of common ionic substances. There are six rules for solubility of salts in water:

1. Most NO_3^- salts are soluble.
2. Most salts of Na^+, K^+, and NH_4^+ are soluble.
3. Most chloride salts are soluble except $AgCl$, $PbCl_2$, and Hg_2Cl_2.
4. Most sulfate salts are soluble except $BaSO_4$, $PbSO_4$, and $CaSO_4$.
5. Most hydroxide salts are only slightly soluble, but important soluble hydroxides are $NaOH$, KOH, and $Ca(OH)_2$.
6. Most sulfide, carbonate, and phosphate salts are only slightly soluble.

Common Ion Effect and Buffers

Buffers are solutions in which the pH remains relatively constant when small amounts of acid or base are added. A buffer is a solution of a weak acid (such as acetic acid, CH_3COOH) and one of its salts (such as its anion, CH_3COO^-). It could also be a solution of a weak base and one of its salts. A buffer solution is better able to resist drastic changes in pH than pure water.

Writing Equations for Chemical Reactions

Chemical reactions involve changes in substances due to the rearrangement of atoms. Bonds are broken and new bonds are formed. Equations use an arrow to the right (→) to indicate a process taking place. No atoms are created or destroyed, thereby obeying the **law of conservation of mass**. Each element has the same number of total atoms on the left of the arrow as it has on the right of the arrow when the equation is balanced.

Some reactants are solids (*s*) which are dissolved in aqueous (*aq*) solution. Some products are precipitates which are solids (*s*). Products which are gases usually are given off into the atmosphere, shown by ↑ or (*g*).

Predicting Reactions: Reaction Types

Synthesis or Combination: Putting together a compound from the elements (A + B → C) or from a compound and an element (A + BC → D). This is a single product from two reactants.

Examples: $N_2 + 3 H_2 \rightarrow 2 NH_3$ OR $ZnS + 2 O_2 \rightarrow ZnSO_4$

Decomposition: The opposite of synthesis – this is the coming apart of a compound into two elements or an element and a compound or two compounds. This is a single reactant with two products: C → A + B

Example 1: $2 H_2O \rightarrow 2 H_2 + O_2$ OR $NH_4NO_3 \rightarrow N_2O + 2 H_2O$

Example 2: $Na_2CO_3 \rightarrow Na_2O + CO_2\uparrow$ OR $MgSO_4 \rightarrow MgO + SO_3$
Decomposition of –ate polyatomic ions results in a metal oxide and water or carbon dioxide or sulfur trioxide.

Single Replacement: This is an element and a compound with the element replacing one of the elements in the compound so that the products are also a compound and an element. A + BC → AC + B
Example: $Zn\,(s) + H_2SO_4\,(aq) \rightarrow ZnSO_4\,(aq) + H_2\uparrow$
A single replacement reaction involving a metal and water yields a metal hydroxide and hydrogen gas: $Ca + 2 H_2O \rightarrow Ca(OH)_2 + H_2\uparrow$

Double Displacement or Double Replacement: This is two compounds switching ions or polyatomic ions and becoming two different compounds. AB + CD → AD + CB

Example: $SrBr_2 + (NH_4)_2CO_3 \rightarrow SrCO_3 + 2 NH_4Br$
Note: Double displacement reactions are not oxidation-reduction reactions.

Combustion: This is a burning by use of oxygen of something usually organic (a combination of carbon and hydrogen) which produces carbon dioxide and water.

Example: $CH_4 + 2 O_2 \rightarrow CO_2 + 2 H_2O$

# Balancing Chemical Equations

1. Determine the correct formulas for all reactants and products, using subscripts to balance ionic charges.
2. Write formulas for reactants on the left of the arrow and predict the products and write their formulas to the right of the arrow.
3. Under the reactants list all the elements in the reactants, starting with metals, then nonmetals, listing oxygen last and hydrogen next to last. Under the products, list all the elements in the same order as those under the reactants (straight across from them).
4. Count the atoms of each element on the left side and list the numbers next to the elements. Repeat for products. Don't forget that subscripts outside a parenthesis multiply everything inside the parenthesis including subscripts inside the parenthesis.
5. For the first element in the list that has unequal numbers of atoms, use a coefficient (numeral to the left of the compound or element) to give the correct number of atoms. NEVER change the subscripts to balance an equation.
6. Go to the next unbalanced element and balance it, moving down the list until all are balanced.
7. Start back at the beginning of the list and actually count the atoms of each element on each side of the arrow to make sure the number listed is the actual number. Rebalance and recheck as needed.

<u>Example</u>: $Al(OH)_3 + NaOH \rightarrow NaAlO_2 + 2\,H_2O$
Al = 1   Al = 1
Na = 1   Na = 1
H = 3 + 1 = 4   H = ~~2~~ 4
O = 3 + 1 = 4   O = ~~2 + 1 = 3~~ 2 + 2 = 4
                Put a 2 in front of H_2O

# Stoichiometry

Stoichiometry is the calculation of theoretical quantities associated with chemical equations. Coefficients and subscripts tell how many atoms there are of each element. Coefficients tell how many moles there are of each element. Chemical equations must obey the **law of conservation of mass** and the **law of conservation of atoms** for each element in the equation in that masses and numbers of atoms of each element must be equal on the two sides of the arrow. (Mass and numbers of atoms cannot be created or lost.)

Stoichiometry can be used to calculate the amount in mass or moles of a product formed from a given mass or moles of a reactant or the amount (mass or moles) of a reactant needed to obtain a specific amount (mass or moles) of a product. As well as mass-mass and mass-mole problems, it can be used for mass-volume, volume-volume, and particle-mass calculations.

The general format is to write the correctly balanced equation with correct formulas. List the "given" information. Then list what is needed. Either start with moles of the given or use the gram formula mass of the given to convert it to moles. Convert moles of given to moles of unknown. Then, if mass of unknown is needed, use the gram formula mass to obtain it from the moles.

Example: How many grams of nitrogen are needed to produce 34.0 g of NH_3?

$$\text{Write Equation: } \underset{?\,g}{N_2} + 3\,H_2 \rightarrow \underset{34.0\,g}{2\,NH_3}$$

Above equation, put givens and unknowns

List what is given and what is unknown:
Mass NH_3: 34.0 g
GFM NH_3: 17.0 g/mol
Moles NH_3: 2 (coefficient)

Mass N_2: unknown
GFM N_2: 28.0 g/mol
Moles N_2: 1 (no coefficient)

Use the label canceling method:

$$34.0\,g\,NH_3 \times \frac{1\,\cancel{mole\,NH_3}}{17.0\,\cancel{g\,NH_3}} \times \frac{1\,\cancel{mole\,N_2}}{2\,\cancel{moles\,NH_3}} \times \frac{28.0\,g\,N_2}{1\,\cancel{mol\,N_2}} =$$

Notice "given" × gfm given × mole ratio × gfm unknown = "unknown"

Because the gfm means that a certain number of grams equals one mole, either the grams can be put on top with the mol on the bottom of the fraction or the mol can be put on top with the grams on the bottom.

In this example, use a calculator to multiply 34.0 times 28.0 (times any other numbers on the top that are not 1) to get 952.0, leave it on the calculator screen, then divide by 17.0 and divide by 2 (if there are any numbers other than 1, divide by those numbers) to get the answer of 28.0 g N_2

If a gas is involved, use 22.4 liters/mol instead of gram formula mass. If the previous example wants the unknown as liters, the last step would be 22.4 L/mol instead of 28.0 g/mol and the answer would be 22.4 liters. If both the given and unknown are expressed in liters, only the mole ratio must be performed since the 22.4 L/1 mol would cancel the 1 mol/22.4 L in the problem. For 34.0 L of NH_3 to be formed, 17.0 L of N_2 would be needed. To get the number of molecules or formula units, use 6.02×10^{23} particles per mol into the equation.

 Limiting Reagent

In a reaction, any reactant that is used up completely is the **limiting reagent**. All reactants that are not used up completely are referred to as being in excess.

Example: What is the maximum number of grams of Cu_2S that can be formed when 80.0 g of Cu reacts with 25.0 g of S?

$$\begin{array}{cccc} & 80.0\text{ g} & 25.0\text{ g} & ?\text{ g} \\ \text{Write Equation:} & 2\text{ Cu} + & \text{S} \rightarrow & Cu_2S \end{array}$$

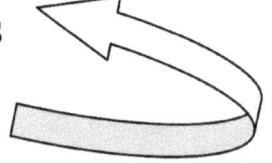

In the equation above, put givens and unknowns.

The problem must be worked twice, once from copper to copper(I) sulfide and once from sulfur to copper(I) sulfide. The amount of copper(I) sulfide produced, the actual answer to the problem, will be the smaller of the numbers obtained.

List what is given and what is unknown:

Mass Cu: 80.0 g
GFM Cu: 63.55 g/mol
Moles Cu: 2 (coefficient)

$MassCu_2S$: unknown
GFM Cu_2S: 159.16 g/mol
Moles Cu_2S: 1 (no coefficient)

Use the label canceling method:

$$80.0\text{ g Cu} \times \frac{1\text{ mole Cu}}{63.55\text{ g Cu}} \times \frac{1\text{ mole }Cu_2S}{2\text{ moles Cu}} \times \frac{159.16\text{ g }Cu_2S}{1\text{ mol }Cu_2S} =$$

Use a calculator to multiply 80.0 times 159.16 to get 12732.8, leave it on the calculator screen, then divide by 63.55 and divide by 2 to get the answer of 100.18 g Cu_2S

List what is given and what is unknown:

Mass S: 25.0 g $MassCu_2S$: unknown
GFM S: 32.06 g/mol   GFM Cu_2S: 159.16 g/mol
Moles S: 1 (no coefficient)   Moles Cu_2S: 1 (no coefficient)

Use the label canceling method:

$$25.0 \text{ g S} \times \frac{1 \text{ mole S}}{32.06 \text{ g S}} \times \frac{1 \text{ mole Cu}_2\text{S}}{1 \text{ moles S}} \times \frac{159.16 \text{ g Cu}_2\text{S}}{1 \text{ mol Cu}_2\text{S}} =$$

Use a calculator to multiply 25.0 times 159.16 to get 3979.0, leave it on the calculator screen, then divide by 32.06 to get the answer of 124.11 g Cu_2S

The 80.0 g of Cu will yield 100.18 g Cu_2S if there is excess S while the 25.0 g S will yield 124.11 g Cu_2S if there is excess Cu. Therefore, since the Cu yields the lesser amount of Cu_2S, it is the limiting reagent and the 100.18 g Cu_2S will be the yield of the reaction.

Theoretical Yield, Actual Yield, and Percent Yield

Using stoichiometry gives the **theoretical yield** of a reaction – that is, the most that the reaction would yield if all conditions were absolutely perfect. However, in reality there is never a time when all the conditions are absolutely perfect, so what is obtained is called the **actual yield**. The ratio of the actual yield to the theoretical yield is called the **percent yield.** It measures the efficiency of the reaction. A percent yield would normally be less than 100%. Reasons for that are that the reaction may reach equilibrium, the reactants may not be pure, there may be error in measurement, or there may be competing side reactions.

$$\text{Percent yield} = \frac{\text{actual yield}}{\text{theoretical yield}} \times 100\%$$

In the reaction in the preceding example, the theoretical yield is 100.18 g Cu_2S. If the reaction was performed in a lab, the lab tech got 89.5 g Cu_2S. Therefore, the percent yield is (89.5/100.18)(100%) = 89.3%.

Oxidation-Reduction Equations and Net Ionic Equations

Oxidation numbers are a method for tracking electrons in a chemical equation. Some ions always have the same oxidation number, but many can change oxidation numbers depending on what other ions are in the compound. The sum of the oxidation numbers (times the subscripts for those ions) of a compound must equal zero. **(1)** To determine oxidation numbers, start by placing the oxidation number above those ions whose oxidation number does not change – any ion from Group 1A is +1, from 2A is +2, from 6A is -2, and from 7A is -1. **(2)** Any uncombined element (listed by itself) is 0. **(3)** Hydrogen is always +1 except in a metal hydride (NaH) when it is -1. **(4)** Oxygen is always -2 except in hydrogen peroxide, H_2O_2, when it is -1. **(5)** In polyatomic ions, the sum of the oxidation numbers must equal the charge on the polyatomic ion.

<u>Example 1</u>: In SO_2, each oxygen is -2, so the net negative charge is -4, giving a net positive charge of +4. Each sulfur is +4.

<u>Example 2</u>: In NH_4^+, each hydrogen is -1 for a total of -4, but the charge on the polyatomic ion is +1, so N must be +5.

<u>Example 3</u>: For $Na_2Cr_2O_7$ the oxygens are -2 each for a total of $(7)(-2) = -14$ and the sodiums are each +1 for a total of $(2)(+1) = +2$. That is a difference of -12. There are 2 chromiums, so $(-12)/(2) = -6$ for each chromium.

The total number of electrons on the left of the equation must equal the total number of electrons on the right. A *decrease* in an element's oxidation number from the left of the arrow (reactants) to the right of the arrow (products) signifies **reduction**. An *increase* in an element's oxidation number left to right signifies **oxidation**. The element undergoing the reduction is reduced and serves as the oxidizing agent (electron acceptor). The element undergoing the oxidation is oxidized and serves as the reducing agent (electron donor). Reduction and oxidation (known as redox) go hand-in-hand in an equation, one cannot happen without the other also happening.

<u>Example 1</u>: In the equation $Cl_2 + 2\ HBr \rightarrow 2\ HCl + Br_2$ both Cl_2 and Br_2 will be zero and H will be +1, making Br^{-1} and Cl^{-1}. That means that chlorine goes from 0 to -1, so it is reduced, and bromine goes from -1 to 0 so it is oxidized.

<u>Example 2</u>: Zinc is oxidized (0 → +2) and manganese is reduced (+4 → +3) in:
$Zn + 2\ MnO_2 + 2\ NH_4Cl \rightarrow ZnCl_2 + Mn_2O_3 + 2\ NH_3 + H_2O$

Balancing redox equations can be tricky, but if the electrons are balanced, the coefficients are easier to balance. Once oxidation numbers have been assigned to all the elements on both sides of the equation and the atoms oxidized and reduced have been identified, use coefficients to make the total increase in oxidation number (loss of electrons) equal to the total decrease in oxidation number (gain of electrons). Then balance the equation as normal.

Example: Ca + 2 H_2O → $Ca(OH)_2$ + H_2
          0   +1 -2   +2 -2 +1   0

Ca: 0 → +2, so add electrons (e-) to right side to make it equal 0
H: +1 → 0, so add electrons to left side to make it equal 0
Ca: 0 → +2 + 2 e-
H: +1 + 1 e- → 0   multiply this half-reaction by 2 so the numbers of electrons are equal, then put that 2 in front of the H_2O

Net ionic reaction: Ca^0 + 2 H_2^{+1} + 1 e- → Ca^{+2} + H_2^0 + 1 e-

Spectator ions are those ions that are unchanged. In this case, O^{-2}.
Now see how close to balanced the equation is:
Ca = 1   Ca = 1
H = 4   H = 2 + 2 = 4
O = 2   O = 2

Half-cell Potentials

An application of redox, half reactions and net ionic reactions is half-cell potentials in batteries and voltaic cells. The flow of electrons causes reduction at the cathode (negatively charged electrode) and oxidation at the anode (positively charged electrode). A cell must be constructed of two half-cells. The electrical potential of a voltaic cell is the ability of the cell to produce an electric current. The standard cell potential (E^0_{cell}) is the measured cell potential when the ion concentrations in the half-cells are $1.00M$, gases are at a pressure of 1 atm, and the temperature is 25° C. Cell potential = $\mathbf{E^0_{cell}}$ = $\mathbf{E^0_{red}}$ - $\mathbf{E^0_{oxid}}$ where E^0_{red} is the reduction potential of the half-cell in which reduction occurs and E^0_{oxid} is the reduction potential of the half-cell in which the oxidation occurs.

Example: Ni(s) + Fe^{2+} (aq) → Ni^{2+} (aq) + Fe(s) and
Half cells: Fe^{3+} + e- → Fe^{2+} $E^0 Fe^{3+}$ = + 0.77 V
              Ni^{2+} + 2 e- → Ni $E^0 Ni^{2+}$ = - 0.25 V

Fe^{3+} is reduced and Ni is oxidized. Since reduction takes place at the Fe^{3+} half-cell, this half-cell is the cathode and since oxidation takes place at the Ni half-cell, this half-cell is the anode. Make sure the two half reactions have the same number of electrons. Use a coefficient for one or both of the half-reactions as necessary.
2 (Fe^{3+} + e- → Fe^{2+}) + (Ni^{2+} + 2 e- → Ni) = 2 Fe^{3+} + Ni^{2+} → 2 Fe^{2+} + Ni
Standard cell potential: E^0_{cell} = E^0_{red} - E^0_{oxid}
E^0_{cell} = + 0.77 V – (-0.25 V) = + 1.02 V

It is possible to predict if a redox reaction will take place spontaneously using standard reduction potentials. The half-reaction with the more positive reduction potential always undergoes reduction while the half-reaction with the less positive reduction potential undergoes oxidation. If the cell potential for the reaction is positive the reaction is spontaneous. If it is negative, the reverse direction of the reaction is spontaneous (and equally positive).

 Gibbs Free Energy, Enthalpy and Entropy

Heat of formation of each element is the heat that is absorbed or released when one mole of the element forms a compound. An **endothermic** reaction takes heat to occur. This is a positive change in heat (+ΔH), so the products have more heat content than the reactants. **Exothermic** reactions give off heat as they occur, so they have a negative change in heat (-ΔH). The products have less heat content than the reactants.

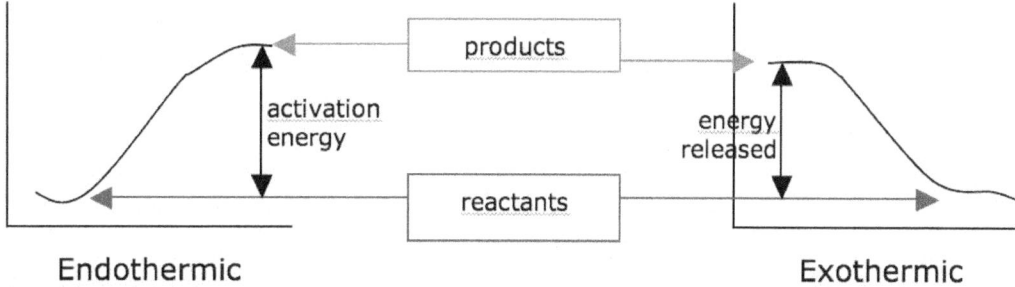

Enthalpy (ΔH) is a measure of the tendency of a reaction toward a more stable compound since it measures the amount of heat a substance has at a given temperature and pressure. If it is negative, the reaction is exothermic and very likely occurs spontaneously.

Calorimetry is the science of measuring heat. **Heat capacity** (C_p) of an element or compound is the measure of how much heat (in Joules) is needed to raise one gram of that substance by one degree Celsius. A simple Styrofoam coffee cup calorimeter can be used in a high school or college laboratory to demonstrate constant pressure calorimetry. The apparatus is two coffee cups (one inside the other for extra insulation), a lid, a stirrer, and a thermometer. If 50.0 mL of HCl (1 mole/liter) at 25.0°C is mixed with 50.0 mL of NaOH (1 mole/liter) at 22.0°C in the calorimeter. After stirring, the temperature is 32.0°C. The specific heat capacity of water is 4.18 J/°C g. The energy released (end product is warmer than the starting reactants) can be calculated by:

$$q = (m)(\Delta T)(C_p)$$

where q is the energy released (in joules), m is the mass of the solution (in grams), and C_p is the specific heat capacity of the substance in question

For HCl: q = (50 mL + 50 mL)(1 g/1mL)(32.0°C - 25.0°C) (4.18 J/°C g)
q = (100 g)(7°C) (4.18 J/°C g)
q = 2926 J for HCl
For NaOH: q = (50 mL + 50 mL)(1 g/1mL)(32.0°C - 22.0°C) (4.18 J/°C g)
q = (100 g)(10°C) (4.18 J/°C g)
q = 4180 J for NaOH
q for the reaction system = 2926 J + 4180 J = 7106 J

For a system where a bar of hot metal was dropped into water to cool it, the $q_{(water)}$ = $q_{(metal)}$ could be used to calculate the mass of the metal. Remember the mass of the system is the mass of the water plus the mass of the metal.

Entropy (ΔS) is a measure of the tendency of a reaction toward more disorder. **Free energy** (ΔG) is dependent on temperature. If free energy is positive, the reaction probably does not occur spontaneously, but if it is negative, the reaction occurs spontaneously. The **Gibbs Free Energy Equation** uses temperature in Kelvin:

$$\Delta G = \Delta H - T \Delta S$$

If ΔH decreases (exothermic) and ΔS increases, the reaction is spontaneous (**exergonic**). The ΔG is negative, so free energy is given off. If ΔH decreases (exothermic) and ΔS decreases, the reaction is spontaneous only if the unfavorable entropy change is offset by a favorable heat content change. If ΔH increases (endothermic) and ΔS increases, the reaction is spontaneous only if the unfavorable heat content change is offset by a favorable entropy change. If ΔH increases (endothermic) and ΔS decreases, the reaction is not spontaneous. The ΔG is positive, so the reaction absorbs free energy, making it **endergonic**.

The heat of formation for an endothermic reaction can be lowered using a catalyst. A catalyst is an element or compound that is added to the reaction to (1) speed the rate of the reaction, (2) make a reaction occur that would not otherwise occur, (3) reduce the minimum activation energy necessary for the reaction to occur, or (4) make a reaction more efficient. When the reaction is finished, the catalyst can be separated out unchanged.

Equilibrium

Many reactions occur with the reactants going completely to products and then the reaction is over (A + B → AB). However, a lot of reactions start with reactants going to products (A + B → AB) and then some of the products break down into reactants (A + B ← AB) while more reactants become products until **equilibrium** of the reaction is attained and maintained. Equilibrium is when the amount of reactants becoming products is equal to the amount of products becoming reactants (A + B ↔ AB). According to **Le Châtelier's Principle,** if a stress is applied to a system in a dynamic equilibrium, the system changes to relieve the stress. Stresses that disturb equilibrium are:

1. Change in concentration – if a reactant's concentration is increased, the equilibrium is displaced to the right (→) meaning that the reactants are used up faster, more products are formed (←), and the new equilibrium has a lower concentration of reactants. Conversely, an increase in a product's concentration displaces the reaction equilibrium to the left, favoring the reactants.
2. Change in pressure – this only applies to gases where an increase in pressure displaces the reaction equilibrium to the right (→)
3. Change in temperature – addition of heat favors the endothermic reaction; however, a rise in temperature increases the rate of any reaction.

Reaction Rates and Rate Laws

In a reaction that goes to completion, the reaction rate depends only on the concentrations of reactants [ ] and is called the **rate law**. The proportionality constant, k, called the rate constant, and n, called the order of the reactant, must both be determined experimentally.

For the reaction $2\,NO_2(g) \rightarrow 2\,NO(g) + O_2(g)$ the rate law is Rate = $k[NO_2]^n$

Given the generalized equilibrium equation: $wA + xB \leftrightarrow yC + zD$ where the lowercase letters represent the coefficients and the capitalized letters represent the reactants (A, B) and the products (C, D), the equilibrium constant, K_{eq}, would be

$$K_{eq} = \frac{[C]^y[D]^z}{[A]^w[B]^x}$$

The square brackets indicate concentrations, usually expressed in molarity.
For the reaction $2\,N_2(g) + 3\,H_2(g) \leftrightarrow 2\,NH_3(g)$

$$K_{eq} = \frac{[NH_3]^2}{[H_2]^3 [N_2]^2}$$

This reaction is second degree with regard to ammonia, second degree with regard to nitrogen, and third degree with regard to hydrogen, making it seventh degree overall.

If K_{eq} is greater than one, the products are favored at equilibrium and if K_{eq} is less than one, the reactants are favored at equilibrium. K_{eq} is also called **solubility product constant**.

Reactant particles must have physical contact (collisions) to transfer electrons or share electrons. The minimum energy those colliding particles need to react is the **activation energy**. At some point enough energy has been put into the colliding particles that they form a complex that is some combination of the reactants and products called an **activated complex** or transitional state. Reactants are converted to products in a single step in an **elementary reaction.**

Most chemical reactions occur by a series of steps called the **reaction mechanism**. An **intermediate** is a product of one reaction that immediately becomes a reactant in another reaction in a multi-step process. The step that creates the activated complex is the **rate limiting step**. The step that is the slowest to happen is the **rate-determining step**. The enthalpy change (ΔH) for a reaction is the sum of the enthalpy changes for the series of reactions that add up to the overall reaction (**Hess's Law**).

Reaction rates are dependent on the number of collisions that take place between particles in a given amount of time. Reaction rates can be <u>increased</u> by:

1. Raising the temperature at which the reaction takes place
2. Increasing the concentration of reactants
3. Increasing surface area of reactant or solute (crushing or powdering)
4. Using a catalyst

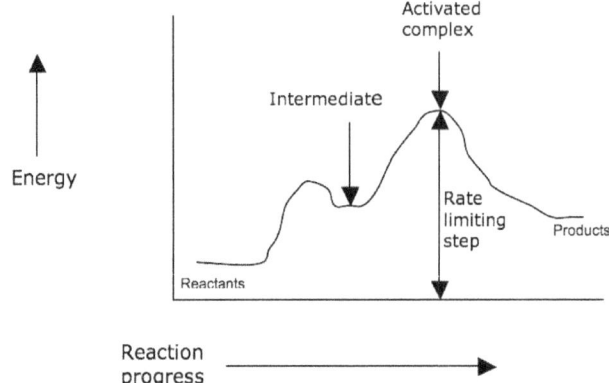

Organic Chemistry

Organic compounds contain carbon which is covalently bonded. **Hydrocarbons** contain only carbon and hydrogen. Organic molecules are the basis of enzymes, proteins, and all living organisms. Most organic compounds do not dissolve in water. Organic compounds are decomposed by heat more easily than most inorganic compounds. Organic reactions generally proceed at much slower rates.

The simplest hydrocarbons are **alkanes** in which every carbon has four bonds, each of which is bonded to another carbon or a hydrogen. Examples are methane, CH_4, and ethane, C_2H_6. Continuous chain alkanes contain any number of carbon atoms in a straight chain. Alkanes are known as saturated hydrocarbons since each bond is a single bond. Alkanes can also have branched chains. Each successive member of the alkane family has the general formula of C_nH_{2n+2}, meaning each increases by CH_2.

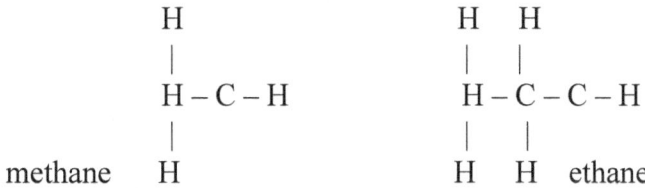

The Latin prefixes used for naming include *meth-* for one carbon, *eth-* for two carbons, *propyl-* for three carbons, *but-* for four carbons, *pent-* for five carbons, *hex-* for six, and *hept-* for seven. If a double or triple bond is present, the number of the beginning carbon is used in the name. The letter "n" at the beginning of a name means normal or straight chain. "Sec" means there is one branch, "iso" means there are two branches from the first carbon, and "tert" means there are two branches from the second carbon. $CH_3(CH_2)_3CH_3$ is n-pentane, $(CH_3)_2CHCH_2CH_3$ is isopentane, $CH_3C(CH_3)_3$ is tert-pentane, and $CH_3CH(CH_3)(CH_2)_2CH_3$ is 2-methylpentane.

A hydrocarbon substituent is called an **alkyl group**. It can be one or more carbons long. Functional group substituents that can be attached to a carbon include hydroxyl (R-OH) to make an alcohol, ether (R-O-R) to make an ether, carbonyl (R-HC=O) to make an aldehyde or (R-RC=O) to make a ketone, carboxyl (R-COOH) to make a carboxylic acid, ester (R-COO-R) to make an ester, and amino (R-NH_2) to make an amine.

To name hydrocarbons find the longest continuous chain of carbons in the molecule. Number the carbons in the main chain in the sequence. Add numbers to the names of the substituent groups to identify their positions on the chain. Use prefixes to indicate the appearance of a group more than once in the structure. List the names of alkyl substituents in alphabetical order. Use proper IUPAC system punctuation. **Stereoisomers** refer to a carbon that has four different groups attached **asymmetrically to a carbon** but still the same molecular structure. They are mirror images.

Alkenes are straight-chain or branched chain hydrocarbons in which two carbon atoms in each molecule are connected by a double covalent bond. Ethylene is C_2H_4 or $H_2C=CH_2$. Successive members of the alkenes have the general formula of C_nH_{2n}.

Geometric isomers differ only in the geometry of their substituted groups. The groups on the carbons of the double bond need not be the same. *Trans* means that the substituted groups are on opposite sides of the double bond while *cis* means the substituted groups are on the same side of the double bond.

trans-2-Pentene

cis-2-Pentene

Alkynes are straight-chain or branched chain hydrocarbons that have at least two carbon atoms in each molecule connected by a triple covalent bond. Acetylene is C_2H_2 while propyne is C_3H_4. Succeeding alkynes add an increment of CH_2. Alkadienes are straight-chain or branched-chain hydrocarbons with two double covalent bonds. They are named by the number of each of the first two carbons in the double bonds and then the Latin prefix for the number of carbons attached to the root word diene. $CH_2=CHCH=CH_2$ is 1,3-butadiene; $CH_2=CH(CH_2)_2CH=CH_2$ is 1,5-hexadiene.

Aromatic hydrocarbons have resonance structures represented by alternate single and double covalent bonds in six-membered carbon rings. The most common is the benzene ring C_6H_6 which is represented by

Nuclear Chemistry

Isotopes are called radioisotopes when they have unstable nuclei that are radioactive.

Alpha particles (α) are positively charged particles (+2) emitted from a radioactive nucleus. They consist of two protons and two neutrons and are identical to the nucleus of a helium atom (^4_2He).

Example: $^{238}_{92}U \rightarrow {}^4_2He + {}^{234}_{90}Th$

When an atom loses an alpha particle, the Z number (atomic number) is lower by two, so move back two spaces on the periodic table to find what the new element is. The new element has an A number (atomic mass number) that is four less than the original element. Because alpha particles are large and heavy, paper or clothing or even dead skin cells shield from their effects.

Beta rays (β) are negatively charged (-1) and fast moving because they are actually electrons. They are written as an electron $^0_{-1}e$ (along with a proton) which is emitted from the nucleus as a neutron decays. Carbon-14 decays by emitting a beta particle.

Example: $^{14}_6C \rightarrow {}^{14}_7N + {}^0_{-1}e$

The Z number actually adds one since its total must be the same on both the left and the right of the arrow and the electron on the right adds a negative one. The A number is unchanged. The Z determines what the element is, so look for it on the periodic table to determine the product. Metal foil or wood is needed to shield from its effects.

Gamma rays (γ) are high energy electromagnetic waves. They are the same kind of radiation as visible light but of much shorter wavelength and higher frequency. Gamma rays have no mass or charge, so the Z and A numbers are not affected. Radioactive atoms often emit gamma rays along with either alpha or beta particles. Protection from gamma radiation takes lead or concrete.

Example 1: $^{226}_{88}Ra \rightarrow {}^{222}_{86}Rn + {}^4_2He + \gamma$

Example 2: $^{234}_{90}Th \rightarrow {}^{234}_{91}Pa + {}^0_{-1}e + \gamma$

A **positron** is a particle with the mass of an electron but a positive charge ($^0_{+1}e$). It may be emitted as a proton changes to a neutron.

Transmutation is the conversion of an atom of one element to an atom of another element such as occurs in alpha and beta radiation. It also occurs when high-energy particles (such as protons, neutrons, or alpha particles) bombard the nucleus of an atom. The elements in the periodic table with atomic numbers above 92 are called the trans-uranium elements, all of which are radioactive elements that have been synthesized in nuclear reactors and nuclear accelerators.

Example: $^{238}_{92}U + ^{1}_{0}n \rightarrow ^{239}_{92}U \rightarrow ^{0}_{-1}e + ^{239}_{93}Np \rightarrow ^{239}_{94}Pu + ^{0}_{-1}e$

Nuclear fission is the splitting of a nucleus into smaller fragments by bombardment with neutrons. Fission releases enormous amounts of energy. Controlled fission is the source of the energy in nuclear power plants. In **nuclear fusion,** hydrogen nuclei fuse to make helium nuclei. Fusion releases even more energy than fission.

Every radioisotope has its own characteristic rate of decay. The **half-life of an isotope** is the time it takes for half the original amount of the isotope in a given sample to decay. For example, the half-life of carbon-14 is 5700 years. If there are 25 grams of carbon-14 in a petrified log, then 5700 years later it will contain 12.5 grams of carbon-14. Another 5700 years later it will contain 6.25 grams of C-14.

About Sample Test Questions

An important note about these test questions. Read before you begin. Our sample test questions are NOT designed to test your knowledge to assess if you are ready to take the test. While all questions WILL test your knowledge, some or all may cover new areas that are not previously covered in this study guide. This is intentional. For questions that you do not answer correctly, take the time to study the question and the answer to prepare yourself for the test.

Sample Test Questions

1) The electron configuration notation for molybdenum is

   A) $1s^2\ 2s^2\ 2p^6\ 3s^2\ 3p^6\ 3d^{10}\ 4s^2\ 4p^6\ 4d^6$
   B) $1s^2\ 2s^2\ 2p^6\ 3s^2\ 3p^6\ 4s^2\ 3d^{10}\ 4p^6\ 3f^6$
   C) $1s^2\ 2s^2\ 2p^6\ 2d^{10}\ 3s^2\ 3p^6\ 3d^{10}\ 3f^4$
   D) $1s^2\ 2s^2\ 2p^6\ 3s^2\ 3p^6\ 4s^2\ 3d^{10}\ 4p^6\ 5s^2\ 4d^4$
   E) $1s^2\ 2s^2\ 3s^2\ 4s^2\ 5s^2\ 2p^6\ 3p^6\ 4p^6\ 3d^{10}\ 4d^4$

The correct answer is D:) $1s^2\ 2s^2\ 2p^6\ 3s^2\ 3p^6\ 4s^2\ 3d^{10}\ 4p^6\ 5s^2\ 4d^4$. The order of filling is 1s 2s 2p 3s 3p 4s 3d 4p 5s 4d 5p 6s 4f 5d 6p 7s 5f 6d 7p with s sublevels holding a maximum of 2 electrons, p holding up to 6, d up to 10 and f up to 14.

2) If a radioactive isotope decays to one half its original mass in three years, what is the total time that will have passed when it reaches one fourth of its original mass?

   A) 4 years
   B) 5.33 years
   C) 6 years
   D) 6.56 years
   E) 7 years

The correct answer is C:) 6 years. From one half its original mass to one fourth its original mass would be a second half-life.

3) The orbital notation for fluorine is

A.

1s²	2s²	2p³	3s²
X	X	\\\	X

B.

1s²	2s²	3p²	2p⁵
X	X	X	XX\

C.

1s²	2s²	2p⁵
X	X	XX\

D.

1s²	2s²	2p³	3s²
X	X	X\	X

E.

1s²	2s²	2p³	3s²
\\	\\	\\\	\\

The correct answer is C:) Two electrons of opposite spin go into the 1s and two electrons of opposite spin go into the 2s, then the 2p fills first with three electrons of the same spin and then with electrons of the opposite spin until enough are there.

4) The pH of a solution measures the acidity or alkalinity of that solution on a scale from zero to fourteen. A solution with a pH of 8 is

  A) Acidic
  B) Basic
  C) Neutral
  D) Ammonia
  E) None of the above

The correct answer is B:) Basic.

5) As the number of neutrons in an atom of a given element increases, its atomic

   A) Number increases
   B) Number decreases
   C) Mass increases
   D) Mass decreases
   E) Number and mass stay the same

The correct answer is C:) Mass increases. The atomic number is the number of protons while the atomic mass is the number of protons and neutrons.

6) Which of the following is composed of hydrocarbon bonds with double bonded carbons?

   A) Ketones
   B) Alkenes
   C) Aldehydes
   D) Amines
   E) None of the above

The correct answer is B:) Alkenes. For example, the basic formula for alkenes is HnC2n.

7) The periodic property which decreases all the way across the table is

   A) Ionization energy
   B) Atomic radius
   C) Ionic size
   D) Shielding effect
   E) Electron affinity

The correct answer is B:) Atomic radius. The atomic radius decreases all the way across the table since adding both protons and electrons going across giving a greater attraction of the electrons by the protons, so it pulls the electrons in tighter to the nucleus.

8) Which of the following elements has the highest ionization energy?

   A) Carbon
   B) Gold
   C) Aluminum
   D) Helium
   E) Tin

The correct answer is D:) Helium. Ionization energy increases as you move from left to right (generally) and top to bottom of the periodic table. Helium has the highest ionization energy of any atom on the periodic table.

9) Which of the following would be expected:

   A) Zinc has a greater shielding effect than calcium
   B) Barium has a greater ionization energy than magnesium
   C) Oxygen has a greater electronegativity than barium
   D) Fluorine has a larger ionic size than iodine
   E) Cesium has a greater electron affinity than sulfur

The correct answer is C:) Oxygen will have a greater electronegativity than barium. Electronegativity increases left to right and decreases going down the periodic table; oxygen has the highest electronegativity of any element.

10) Which of the following affects boiling point?

   I. Pressure
   II. Intermolecular forces
   III. Purity of the substance

   A) I and II only
   B) I and III only
   C) II and III only
   D) I only
   E) I, II and III

The correct answer is E:) I, II and III. Each of the three factors have an effect on the boiling and melting point of a substance.

11) If 88.0% of the atoms of an element have a mass of 28.0 amu, 9.0% have a mass of 29.0 amu, and the rest have a mass of 30.0 amu, what is the average atomic mass?

   A) 28.15 amu
   B) 27.25 amu
   C) 24.64 amu
   D) 45.0 amu
   E) 31.8 amu

The correct answer is A:) 28.15 amu
Average atomic mass = $(0.88)(28.0) + (0.09)(29.0) + (0.03)(30.0) =$
$\quad\quad\quad\quad\quad\quad\quad\quad\quad\quad$ 24.64 $\quad + \quad$ 2.61 $\quad + \quad$ 0.90 $\quad$ = 28.15 amu

12) The sodium ion consists of

   A) 11 protons, 11 neutrons, 11 electrons
   B) 12 protons, 11 neutrons, 12 electrons
   C) 11 protons, 12 neutrons, 10 electrons
   D) 12 protons, 11 neutrons, 10 electrons
   E) 10 protons, 11 neutrons, 11 electrons

The correct answer is C:) 11 protons, 12 neutrons, and 10 electrons. Sodium's atomic number is 11 so it has 11 protons. Its atomic mass is 22.99 so it has 22.99 − 11 = 11.99 or 12 neutrons. As an atom, it is neutral so it has the same number of electrons as protons, but as an ion, it loses the $3s^1$ electron, giving it 11 − 1 = 10 electrons.

13) According to modern methods of naming binary compounds, the name for P_4S_3 is

   A) Phosphoric sulfide
   B) Phosphorus (IV) sulfur (III)
   C) Phosphorus sulfide
   D) Phosphorus trisulfide
   E) Tetraphosphorus trisulfide

The correct answer is E:) Tetraphosphorus trisulfide. It is made of two nonmetals, so the number of atoms of each element must be specified.

14) Which of the following describes the similarities of families on the periodic table?

   A) They have the same configuration of electrons on their outer shells.
   B) They have the same atomic mass.
   C) They have the same levels of radioactivity.
   D) They have similar levels of electronegativity and polarity.
   E) None of the above

The correct answer is A:) They have the same configurations of electrons on their outer shells. Families are also called groups and are the vertical columns on the table.

15) Copper (II) phosphate is

   A) Cu_2PO_4
   B) $Cu_3(PO_4)_2$
   C) $Cu_2(PO_4)_3$
   D) $CuPO_4$
   E) Cu_3PO_8

The correct answer is B:) $Cu_3(PO_4)_2$. Copper (II) has a charge of +2 and phosphate (PO_4) has a charge of -3. Since it has to be neutral, three ions of Cu^{+2} are needed and two polyatomic ions of PO_4^{-3} are needed.

16) Which piece of equipment should be used to measure 50mL?

   A) Meter stick
   B) Triple beam balance
   C) Graduated cylinder
   D) Overflow bucket
   E) None of the above

The correct answer is C:) Graduated cylinder. 50mL is a volume amount of a liquid. This would be best measured using a graduated cylinder.

17) A helium nucleus emitted from the nucleus of a radioactive nuclide is called a(n)

   A) Alpha particle
   B) Beta particle
   C) Positron
   D) Neutron
   E) Gamma ray

The correct answer is A:) alpha particle. An alpha particle is $_4^2 He$.

18) Which of the following orbitals has four balloon shaped areas which arrange themselves so they seem to be pointing to the corners of a tetrahedron?

   A) sp3
   B) s
   C) ssp1
   D) p2p
   E) sp

The correct answer is A:) sp3. This is a hybrid of the s and p orbitals.

19) What much of a 1600 gram sample of $^{68}_{32}$Ge, whose half-life is about nine months, will remain after 4.5 years?

   A) 4 ½ grams
   B) 25 grams
   C) 50 grams
   D) 30 grams
   E) 267 grams

The correct answer is B:) 25 grams. Four and a half years times twelve months is fifty-four months. 54 months divided by 9 months is 6 half-lives. Therefore, at the end of the first half-life (9 months), there is 800 grams. After the second (18 months), 400 grams. After the third (27 months), 200 grams. After the fourth (36 months), 100 grams, and after the fifth (45 months) 50 grams. And after the sixth half-life (54 months) there is 25 grams left.

20) Which of the following could be an alkene?

   A) H2C
   B) CN2H
   C) H2C4
   D) N4H3C2
   E) None of the above

The correct answer is C:) H2C4. A general formula for alkenes is HnC2n. Alkenes are composed of hydrocarbons, or hydrogen and carbon bonds.

21) The release of a beta particle by $^{14}_{6}$C results in

   A) No change to the carbon
   B) $^{14}_{7}$N
   C) $^{14}_{5}$B
   D) $^{16}_{8}$O
   E) $^{14}_{7}$C

The correct answer is B:) $^{14}_{7}$N. $^{14}_{6}$C $\rightarrow$ $^{14}_{7}$N + $^{0}_{-1}$e.

22) The gram formula mass of $(NH_4)_2SO_4$ is

   A) 74 grams
   B) 118 grams
   C) 64 grams
   D) 114 grams
   E) 132 grams

The correct answer is E:) 132 grams. 2 N + 2 (4 H) + S + 4 O = 2(14) + 8(1) + 1(32) + 4(16) = 28 + 8 + 32 + 64 = 132 grams

23) Which of the following best describes a metallic bond?

   A) Free flow of electrons among bonded elements.
   B) A structured and rigid bond between elements.
   C) Sharing patterns of electrons amongst elements.
   D) Attractions among elements, but without bonding.
   E) None of the above

The correct answer is A:) Free flow of electrons among bonded elements.

24) Approximately how many moles of atoms are there in 48.09 grams of sulfur?

   A) 16.03 moles
   B) 0.667 moles
   C) 1.50 moles
   D) 9.10×10^{23} moles
   E) 1541.77 moles

The correct answer is C:) 1.50 moles. 48.09 g S x 1 mole S / 32.06 g S = 1.50 moles

25) If an initial burette reading is 1.8 mL and the final reading is 9.6 mL, which of the following occurred?

   A) 7.8 mL were added
   B) 7.8 mL were removed
   C) A chemical reaction
   D) The burette cracked
   E) None of the above

The correct answer is B:) 7.8 mL were removed. The readings on a buret read from bottom to top, therefore liquid must have been removed for the reading to increase.

26) What is the number of molecules of iron(III) bromide in 0.492 grams of iron(III) bromide?

A) 2.18×10^{21} molecules
B) 2.96×10^{23} molecules
C) 6.02×10^{23} molecules
D) 1.00×10^{21} molecules
E) 10.00×10^{21} molecules

The correct answer is D:) 1.00×10^{21} molecules. Iron(III) bromide is $FeBr_3$. Its gram formula mass is (1 mol Fe)(55.85 g Fe / 1 mol Fe) + (3 mol Br)(79.90 g Br / 1 mol Br) = 55.85 g + 239.70 g = 295.55 g / mol $FeBr_3$. Start with what you are looking for: (6.02×10^{23} molecules / 1 mol) (1 mol $FeBr_3$ / 295.55 g $FeBr_3$)(0.495 g $FeBr_3$) = 1.00×10^{21} molecules

27) Which of the following best describes how to filter solid precipitate from a liquid?

A) Give the precipitate time to settle at the bottom of a beaker and then manually dump out all of the liquid.
B) Use a suction filtration system by setting up a funnel with a filter paper over a filter flask, and attach a suctioning force to the extra opening pulling the liquid down and causing the precipitate to get caught in the filter paper.
C) Introduce a chemical which will cause the liquid to disappear and leave behind only the original precipitate.
D) Both B and C are correct.
E) None of the above are correct.

The correct answer is B:) Use a suction filtration system by setting up a funnel with a filter paper over a filter flask, and attach an aspirator to the extra opening pulling the liquid down and causing the precipitate to get caught in the filter paper. The aspirator sucks the air out of the tube which pulls the liquid down. If there is solid precipitate it will get caught in the filter paper.

28) What is the density of UF_6?

   A) 22.4 liters
   B) 352 grams
   C) 15.45 grams
   D) 352 grams/mole
   E) 15.45 grams/liter

The correct answer is E:) 15.45 grams/liter. Gram formula mass for UF_6 is (1)(238.03 grams U / 1 mole U) + (6)(18.00 grams F / 1 mole F) = 238.03 grams / mol + 108 grams / mol = 346.03 grams/mol UF_6. Density is expressed in grams/liter, so divide gfm by 22.4 liters/mol. (346.03 grams / mol) / (22.4 l / mol) = 15.45 g/l

29) Which of the following describes electronegativity?

   A) The strength it takes to remove a valence electron from an atom.
   B) The strength with which an electron pulls on shared electrons in a covalent bond.
   C) The total energy change of a neutral atom when an electron is added to it.
   D) The strength with which the electron resists an increase in atomic mass.
   E) None of the above

The correct answer is B:) The strength with which an electron pulls on shared electrons in a covalent bond. Electronegativity increases the farther right and closer to the top of the periodic table an element is.

30) Calculate the empirical formula for the compound formed when 0.923 grams of sodium combines with hydrogen to produce 0.963 grams of compound.

   A) Na_2H
   B) H_2N_a
   C) NaH
   D) Na_2H_2
   E) NaH_2

The correct answer C:) NaH. 0.923 g Na and 0.963 – 0.923 g H = 0.040 g H. Percent composition is (0.923/0.963)(100%) = 95.8% Na and (0.040/0.963)(100%) = 4.2%H. To convert percentages to moles: For Na, (95.8 g Na)(1 mol Na / 23 g Na) = 4.17 or 4.2 mol Na. For H, (4.2 g H)(1 mol H / 1 g H) = 4.2 mol H for a 1:1 ratio or NaH.

31) Ascorbic acid, also known as vitamin C, has a percentage composition of 40.9% carbon, 4.58% hydrogen, and 54.5% oxygen. Its molecular mass is 176.1 grams. What is its molecular formula?

   A) CH_2O
   B) $C_2H_2O_4$
   C) $C_3H_4O_3$
   D) $C_6H_8O_6$
   E) CHO_2

The correct answer is D:) $C_6H_8O_6$. Convert percentages to moles: (40.9 gC)(1 mol C/12 gC) = 3.41 mol C(4.58 g H)(1 mol H/1 g H) = 4.58 mol H
(54.5 g O)(1 mol O/16 g O) = 3.41 mol O The C:O ratio is 1:1, but the C:H or O:H ratio is 3.41:4.58 which makes it 4.58/3.41 = 1.34 so all have to be multiplied by 3 to get the whole numbers of C:H:O = $C_3H_4O_3$ for an empirical formula. The mass of $C_3H_4O_3$ is (3)(12 g C/1 molC) + (4)(1 g H/1 mol H) + (3)(16 g O/1 mol O) = 36 g/mol C + 4 g/mol H + 48 g/mol O = 88 g/mol for $C_3H_4O_3$. The molecular mass/empirical mass = 176.1 g/88 g = 2, so multiply the subscripts by 2.

32) If a series of atoms are bonded together and they are electroneutral, which of the following is true?

   A) There is exactly 7 atoms
   B) They are all exactly the same size
   C) They are ionized
   D) They have no charge
   E) None of the above

The correct answer is D:) They have no charge. Electroneutral means there is no charge.

33) Oxygen is one of the most active elements as would be expected from its

   A) Low ionization energy
   B) High electronegativity
   C) High atomic radius
   D) Low polarity
   E) High ionization energy

The correct answer is B:) High electronegativity. The higher the electronegativity, the more reactive the element.

34) Which of the following has 1 sigma and 1 pi bond?

    A) N:::N
    B) O:N
    C) C:::O
    D) N:C
    E) O::O

The correct answer is E:) O::O. A single bond is a sigma bond. When period 2 elements form increased bonds (such as in the answer) they also form pi bonds. A double bond is one sigma bond and one pi bond.

35) The compound that contains 50% of each element by mass is

    A) CO
    B) CO_2
    C) Na_2O_2
    D) SO_2
    E) H_2O

The correct answer is D:) SO_2. The mass of S = 32 g/mole and the mass of O_2 is (2)(16 g/mole) = 32 g/mole.

36) Which of the following is NOT a functional group?

    A) Alcohol
    B) Aldehyde
    C) Carboxylic Acid
    D) Amine
    E) All of the above are functional groups

The correct answer is E:) All of the above are functional groups. Other functional groups include amide, ester and ketone.

37) In a balanced equation, the relative numbers of moles of the reactants used and products formed are given by

    A) Subscripts within parentheses
    B) Coefficients of the formulas
    C) Subscripts outside the parentheses
    D) Superscripts of the formulas
    E) A multiplication of coefficients by subscripts

The correct answer is B:) Coefficients of the formulas. Subscripts balance formulas; coefficients balance equations.

38) Dipole moment is a measure of

   A) Electronegativity
   B) Polarity
   C) Ionization
   D) Electron affinity
   E) None of the above

The correct answer is B:) Polarity. Polarity is when the electrons group to one side of a bond, causing one half to be charged slightly positively and one half to be charged slightly negatively.

39) The algebraic sum of the oxidation numbers of the atoms in the formula of a radical is equal to its

   A) Charge
   B) Valence
   C) Positive charge
   D) Negative charge
   E) Number of moles

The correct answer is A:) Charge. Some of the oxidation numbers will be positive and some will be negative, so when those are added together the resulting number (positive or negative) will be the charge on the radical.

40) Products which are insoluble and leave the reaction environment are

   A) Perceptions
   B) Salts
   C) Precepts
   D) Masses
   E) Precipitates

The correct answer is E:) Precipitates. A precipitate is a solid substance formed as a product of the reactants. It is insoluble in that environment and drops to the bottom of the beaker. It can be a salt, but is not always a salt. It is usually crystalline.

41) Which of the following is correct?

    A) $N_2 + 6H \rightarrow 2NH_3$
    B) $2N + 3H_2 \rightarrow 2NH_3$
    C) $N + 3H \rightarrow NH_3$
    D) $N_2 + 3H_2 \rightarrow 2NH_3$
    E) $N_2 + 1½H_2 \rightarrow 2NH_3$

The correct answer is D:) $N_2 + 3H_2 \rightarrow 2NH_3$. Synthesis reaction of nitrogen and hydrogen to form ammonia. Nitrogen and hydrogen are diatomic, N_2 and H_2, so cannot be single atoms of elements. Coefficients must be whole numbers. There must be two nitrogen atoms on each side of the arrow which means the six hydrogen atoms on the right must be balanced with six on the left.

42) Barium carbonate, when heated, yields

    A) Barium carbide and water
    B) Barium and carbon trioxide
    C) Barium carbide and oxygen
    D) Barium and carbon dioxide
    E) Barium oxide and carbon dioxide

The correct answer is E:) Barium oxide and carbon dioxide. Decomposition of a carbonate: $Ba(CO_3) \rightarrow BaO + CO_2$

43) Aluminum + iron(III) oxide $\rightarrow$

    A) $Al_2(Fe_2O_3)_3$
    B) $Al_2O_3 + Fe$
    C) $Al_2O_3 + 2Fe$
    D) $Al_3O_2 + Fe$
    E) $AlO + Fe_3$

The correct answer is C:) $Al_2O_3 + 2Fe$. Single replacement reaction: $2Al + Fe_2O_3 \rightarrow Al_2O_3 + 2Fe$

44) $2\,Na + 2\,H_2O \rightarrow$

    A) $2\,NaOH + O_2\uparrow$
    B) $2\,Na_2O + H_2\uparrow$
    C) $Na_2OH + H_2\uparrow$
    D) $Na(OH)_2 + H_2\uparrow$
    E) $2\,NaOH + H_2\uparrow$

The correct answer is E:) $2\,NaOH + H_2\uparrow$. A single replacement reaction involving water gives a hydroxide and hydrogen gas.

45) Ammonium sulfide + iron(II) nitrate $\rightarrow$

    A) $NH_4NO_3 + FeS$
    B) $2\,NH_4NO_3 + FeS$
    C) $2\,NH_3NO_3 + Fe_3S_2$
    D) $2\,NH_4NO_3 + Fe_2S_3$
    E) $(NH_4)2NO_3 + FeS$

The correct answer is B:) $2\,NH_4NO_3 + FeS$. Double displacement reaction: $(NH_4)_2S + Fe(NO_3)_2 \rightarrow 2\,NH_4NO_3 + FeS$

46) If 16 liters of carbon monoxide is burned to form carbon dioxide, how many liters of oxygen will be required and how many liters of carbon dioxide will be produced?

    A) 16 L O_2 and 16 L CO_2
    B) 16 L O_2 and 32 L CO_2
    C) 8 L O_2 and 24 L CO_2
    D) 8 L O_2 and 8 L CO_2
    E) 8 L O_2 and 16 L CO_2

The correct answer is E:) 8 L O_2 and 16 L CO_2. The balanced equation: $2\,CO + O_2 \rightarrow 2\,CO_2$ 16 liters CO x 1 mol O_2/2 mol CO = 8 liters O_2 16 liters CO x 2 mol CO_2/2 mol CO = 16 liters CO_2

47) For the reaction of 7.0 moles of aluminum and 8.0 moles of chlorine, which will be the limiting reagent and by how much?

A) Chorine by 5.33 moles
B) Aluminum by 5.33 moles
C) Chlorine by 1.67 moles
D) Aluminum by 1.67 moles
E) Neither one is limiting

The correct answer is C:) Chlorine by 1.67 moles. The balanced equation: $2\ Al + 3\ Cl_2 \rightarrow 2\ AlCl_3$, 7.0 mol Al x (2 mol $AlCl_3$/2 mol Al) = 7.0 mol $AlCl_3$, 8.0 mol Cl_2 x (2 mol $AlCl_3$/3 mol Cl_2) = 5.33 mol $AlCl_3$ Chlorine is the limiting reagent by 7.0 – 5.33 = 1.67 moles

48) Calcium carbonate can be decomposed by heating. What is the percent yield of this reaction if 24.8 grams of $CaCO_3$ is heated to give 13.1 grams of CaO?

A) 94.2%
B) 92.4%
C) 106.1%
D) 47.2%
E) 89.3%

The correct answer is A:) 94.2%. To calculate the theoretical yield, start with a balanced equation: $CaCO_3 \rightarrow CaO + CO_2$ 24.8 g $CaCO_3$ x 1 mol $CaCO_3$/100.08 g $CaCO_3$ x 1 mol/1mol CaO x 56.08 g CaO/1 mol CaO = 13.90 g CaO Percent yield = actual yield/theoretical yield x 100% Percent yield = 13.1 g/13.9 g x 100% = 94.2%

49) Hydrazine, N_2H_4, is used as a rocket fuel. It reacts with oxygen to form nitrogen and water: $N_2H_4\ (l) + O_2(g) \rightarrow N_2(g) + 2\ H_2O(g)$ How many liters of N2 (at STP) form when 1.0 kg of N_2H_4 reacts with 1.0 kg O_2?

A) 0.70 L N_2
B) 0.746 L N_2
C) 46.17 L N_2
D) 700.0 L O_2
E) 700.0 L N_2

The correct answer is E:) 700.0 L N_2. 1.0 kg N_2H_4 x (1000 g N_2H_4/1.0 kg N_2H_4) x (1 mol N_2H_4/30.02 g N_2H_4) x (1 mol N_2/1 mol N_2H_4) x (22.4 L N_2/1 mol N_2) = 746.17 L N_2 1.0 kg O_2 x (1000 g O_2/1.0 kg O_2) x (1 mol O_2/32.00 g O_2) x (1 mol N_2/1 mol O_2) x (22.4 L N_2/1mol N_2) = 700.0 L N_2 - limiting - what is produced

50) A blacksmith heated an iron bar to 1450° C. The blacksmith then tempered the metal by dropping it into 43,000 cm³ of water that had a temperature of 22° C. The final temperature of the system was 45° C. What was the mass of the bar? (C_p of iron = 0.4494 J/g°C and C_p of water is 4.18 J/g°C)

  A) 6500.0 g
  B) 1566.0 g
  C) 5682.5 g
  D) 2969.5 g
  E) 1511.3 g

The correct answer is C:) 5682.5 g. q = (m)(ΔT)(Cp) and q for iron = q for water (heat lost by iron = heat gained by water) The mass of the system is (43,000 g + m) – remember 1 cm³ = 1 g (43,000 g + m)(45-22°C)(4.18 J/g°C) = m(1450-45°C)(0.4494 J/g°C) 4,134,020 g + 96.14m = -631.40m OR 4,134,020 g = -727.5m

51) An activated complex

  A) Is a transitional state
  B) Occurs in all reactions
  C) Is the result of new bonds
  D) Results in activation energy
  E) Is all about broken bonds

The correct answer is A:) Is a transitional state. An activated complex is called the transition state. It is a group of atoms on the way to becoming an ionic or molecular product. An activated complex is the arrangement of atoms at the peak of the activation energy barrier.

52) In the equilibrium reaction, rA + sB ↔ tC + uD, the ratio of products to the reactants is NOT

  A) K_{eq}
  B) [A][B] / [C][D]
  C) $[C]^t [D]^u / [A]^r [B]^s$
  D) Dependent on the initial concentrations of A and B
  E) An indicator of whether products or reactants are favored at equilibrium

The correct answer is B:) [A][B] / [C][D]. If C is true, B cannot be true.

53) For the hypothetical reaction, A + B ↔ C + D, an increase in the concentration of A will

   A) Displace the equilibrium to the left
   B) Cause A and B to be used up faster
   C) Cause more C but not D to be formed
   D) Result in a reestablished equilibrium in which A is used completely
   E) Cause the activation energy to be lower

The correct answer is B:) Cause A and B to be used up faster. If [A] is increased, the equilibrium is displaced to the right, causing more of B to be used and A and B to be used faster, thereby forming more C and D. It does not affect activation energy.

54) In the synthesis of ammonia, an increase in pressure will result in a greater yield of ammonia because

   A) The formation of ammonia molecules tends to relieve the pressure
   B) Hydrogen has a lower molecular mass than nitrogen
   C) There are two molecules of ammonia formed for every four molecules of reactants used
   D) Ammonia has a lower molecular mass than nitrogen
   E) A higher temperature

The correct answer is A:) The formation of ammonia molecules tends to relieve the pressure. Increasing the pressure in a system forces the reaction toward the products.

55) A certain solution is found to contain 0.00001 mole of H_3O^+ per liter. Its pH is

   A) 0.00001
   B) 1×10^{-5}
   C) 5
   D) -5
   E) 9

The correct answer is C:) 5. 0.00001 = 1.0×10^{-5} mol/L which is a pH of 5

56) $Ca(OH)_2$ is a(n)

   A) Arrhenius acid
   B) A salt
   C) Lewis acid
   D) Precipitate
   E) Arrhenius base

The correct answer is E:) Arrhenius base. Arrhenius bases have to have OH^- in them.

57) In the reaction $HNO_3 + H_2O \leftrightarrow H_3O^+ + NO_3^-$, which is NOT true?

   A) HNO_3 & NO_3^- are a conjugate acid-base pair
   B) H_2O & H_3O^+ are a conjugate acid-base pair
   C) H_2O is a hydrogen acceptor
   D) H_2O is a base
   E) H_2O is an acid

The correct answer is E:) H_2O is an acid. HNO_3 donates a H^+ so it is an acid and pairs with NO_3^- as an acid-base pair. H_2O accepts a H^+ so it is a base and pairs with H_3O^+ as an acid-base pair.

58) An isotope is an element with

   A) A different number of neutrons and the same number of protons in each atom.
   B) A different number of protons and the same number of neutrons in each atom.
   C) An equal number of protons and neutrons in each atom.
   D) The same number of protons and neutrons and a different number of electrons in each atom.
   E) None of the above.

The correct answer is A:) A different number of neutrons and the same number of protons in each atom.

59) _____ is the moles of solute per kilogram of solvent. _____ is moles of solute per liter of solution.

   A) Polarity, Molarity
   B) Molarity, Molality
   C) Molality, Polarity
   D) Molality, Molarity
   E) None of the above

The correct answer is D:) Molality, Molarity.

60) In the equation, $K_2Cr_2O_7 + H_2O + S \rightarrow KOH + Cr_2O_3 + SO_2$, the chromium ion makes what oxidation number change?

A) +5 to +3
B) +6 to +2
C) +12 to +6
D) +6 to +3
E) +2 to +3

The correct answer is D:) +6 to +3. In $K_2Cr_2O_7$ the K is +1 (total +2) and the O is -2 (total -14), so the total Cr is +12, making each a +6. In Cr_2O_3 the O is -2 (total -6), so the Cr total is + 6, making each Cr +3.

61) How many milliliters of 0.28M $K_2Cr_2O_7$ are needed to reduce 1.40 g of sulfur in the equation in # 43 (when balanced)?

A) 156.3 mL
B) 104.2 mL
C) 2000 mL
D) 30,645.8 mL
E) 2,402.6 mL

The correct answer is B:) 104.2 mL. Balanced equation: $2 K_2Cr_2O_7 + 2 H_2O + 3 S \rightarrow 4 KOH + 2 Cr_2O_3 + 3 SO_2$ (1.40 g S)(1 mol S/32.0 g S)(2 mol $K_2Cr_2O_7$ / 3 mol S)(1L $K_2Cr_2O_7$/0.28 mol $K_2Cr_2O_7$)(1000 mL/1L) = 104.2 mL

62) What are the correct coefficients in the correct order for this redox equation: $HNO_3 + H_2S \rightarrow S + NO + H_2O$

A) 1, 1, 1, 2, 1
B) 2, 1, 1, 2, 1
C) 2, 1, 1, 1, 2
D) 2, 1, 1, 2, 2
E) 2, 3, 3, 2, 4

The correct answer is E:) 2, 3, 3, 2, 4. In HNO_3, H = +1, O = -2 (total -6), so N = +5. In H_2S, H = +1 and S = -2. On the right, S = 0. If O = -2, then N = +2. In H_2O, H = +1 and O = -2. The two half-reactions are: $N^{+5} \rightarrow N^{+2}$ and $S^{-2} \rightarrow S^0$. By adding 3 e- to N^{+5} and 2 e- to S^0 the half-reactions are: $N^{+5} + 3$ e- $\rightarrow N^{+2}$ and $S^{-2} \rightarrow S^0 + 2$ e- so the N's must be multiplied by 2 and the S's by 3. The balanced equation: $2 HNO_3 + 3 H_2S \rightarrow 3 S + 2 NO + 4 H_2O$

Use this equation to answer the next three questions:
$$2\ Sb(s) + HNO_3(aq) \rightarrow Sb_2O_5(s) + NO(g) + H_2O(l)$$

63) What element is oxidized?

   A) Sb
   B) H
   C) N
   D) O
   E) None

The correct answer is A:) Sb. $Sb^0 \rightarrow Sb_2^{+5}$ Oxidation shows an increase in oxidation number.

64) What is the oxidizing agent?

   A) Sb
   B) HNO_3
   C) H
   D) N
   E) O

The correct answer is B:) HNO_3 $N^{+5} \rightarrow N^{+2}$ Nitrogen is reduced. The compound containing the element which is reduced is the oxidizing agent.

65) What is the reducing agent?

   A) Sb
   B) HNO_3
   C) H
   D) N
   E) O

The correct answer is A:) Sb. The element which is oxidized is the reducing agent.

66) The volume of a particular amount of dry gas is inversely proportional to the pressure, provided the temperature remains constant is

   A) Charles' Law
   B) Boyle's Law
   C) Kelvin's Law
   D) LeChatelier's Principle
   E) James' Law

The correct answer is B:) Boyle's Law. Boyle's Law states that for a given mass of gas at constant temperature, the volume of the gas varies inversely with pressure.

67) Given 700 mL of oxygen at 7° C and 80.0 cm pressure, what volume does it have at 27° C and 50.0 cm pressure?

   A) 469 mL
   B) 1045 mL
   C) 1200 mL
   D) 4320 mL
   E) 0.112 mL

The correct answer is C:) 1200 mL. $P_1V_1T_2 = P_2V_2T_1$ (80.0 cm)(700 mL)(27 + 273) = (50.0 cm)(x)(7 + 273) (1.68 x 10^7) = (1.40 x 10^4) (x) 1200 mL = x

68) A volume of 50.0 mL of gas is collected over mercury at 17° C and 760 mm pressure. The mercury level inside the eudiometer is 30.0 mm higher than that outside. What volume will the gas occupy at STP?

   A) 45.3 mL
   B) 46.1 mL
   C) 51.1 mL
   D) 49.1 mL
   E) 43.5 mL

The correct answer is A:) 45.3 mL. $P_1V_1T_2 = P_2V_2T_1$ (760 mm)(50.0mL)(273 K) = (760 + 30.0mm)(V$_2$)(273 + 17 K) 1,0374,000 = (229,100) (V$_2$) 45.28 mL = (V$_2$)

69) An ion is an atom with

   A) A positive charge
   B) A negative charge
   C) An equal number of protons and electrons
   D) An unequal number of protons and electrons
   E) None of the above

The correct answer is D:) An unequal number of protons and electrons.

70) If the K_a for oxalic acid is 5.6×10^{-2}, for acetic acid is 1.8×10^{-5}, and for benzoic acid is 6.3×10^{-5}, rank the three acids from strongest to weakest.

   A) Oxalic, acetic, benzoic
   B) Acetic, benzoic, oxalic
   C) Oxalic, benzoic, acetic
   D) Benzoic, oxalic, acetic
   E) Acetic, oxalic, benzoic

The correct answer is C:) oxalic, benzoic, acetic. Oxalic: $1.25 = -\log 5.6 \times 10^{-2}$; benzoic: $4.20 = -\log 6.3 \times 10^{-5}$; acetic: $4.74 = -\log 1.8 \times 10^{-5}$

71) An acid with a molarity of 6.0 M is a

   A) Strong acid
   B) Concentrated acid
   C) Weak acid
   D) Dilute acid
   E) Neutral solution

The correct answer is D:) Dilute acid. If it is 6.0 mol/L, that means its pH is 1×10^{-6}, so it is near neutral which is dilute.

Use the following information for the next four questions:

$H_2 (g) + \frac{1}{2} O_2 (g) \rightarrow H_2O (g)$ performed electrically using $Pt/H_2(g)/H^+ \parallel H_2O/O_2(g)/Pt$

Half cells: $H_2 \rightarrow 2 H^+ + 2 e^-$ $E^0 = {}^+ 0.00$ V
$O_2 + 4 H^+ + 4 e^- \rightarrow 2 H_2O$ $E^0 = {}^+ 1.23$ V

72) This half-reaction $H_2 \rightarrow 2 H^+ + 2 e^-$ indicates:

A) Reduction at the anode
B) Oxidation at the anode
C) Reduction at the cathode
D) Oxidation at the cathode
E) Both oxidation and reduction

The correct answer is B:) Oxidation at the anode. H_2 is going from 0 → +1 so it is being oxidized at the anode

73) Calculate the standard cell potential.

A) ⁻1.23 V
B) ⁺1.23 V
C) 0.00 V
D) ⁻2.46 V
E) ⁺0.615

The correct answer is B:) ⁺1.23 V. ⁺0.00 V + ⁺1.23 V = ⁺1.23 V

74) Standard entropies in J/K-mol are: $H_2 (g) = 130.6$, $H_2O (g) = 188.7$, and $O_2 (g) = 205.0$. Calculate the change in entropy for the reaction.

A) – 46.9 J/K
B) – 88.8 J/K
C) + 44.4 J/K
D) – 66.6 J/K
E) – 44.4 J/K

The correct answer is E:) – 44.4 J/K. $\Delta S°$ (reaction) = S° (products) - S° (reactants) = (1 mole)(188.7 J/K-mol) – [(1 mole)(130.6 J/K-mol) + (½ mole)(205.0 J/K-mol)] = 188.7 – (130.6 + 102.5) = 188.7 – 233.1 = – 44.4 J/K

75) The platinum in this reaction does NOT

   A) Increase the rate of the reaction.
   B) Interfere with the reaction.
   C) Catalyze the reaction.
   D) Lower the activation energy barrier.
   E) Get recovered at the end.

The correct answer is B:) Interfere with the reaction. Platinum is a catalyst in this reaction, so it does increase the rate of the reaction, lower its activation energy barrier, and get recovered at the end of the reaction.

76) In the reaction $HCl + NaOH \rightarrow NaCl + H_2O$

   A) NaCl will be a precipitate
   B) NaCl will dissociate
   C) Na+ will be a spectator ion
   D) NaCl will be an acid
   E) H_2O will be a base

The correct answer is A:) NaCl will be a precipitate. This is an acid-base reaction resulting in a precipitated salt and water.

77) In the case of liquids dissolved in liquids, little change in temperature is expected because

   A) Only a small amount of solute can dissolve
   B) All liquids are completely miscible
   C) No change in physical state occurs
   D) Hydration prevents chemical activity
   E) Liquids don't dissolve

The correct answer is C:) No change in physical state occurs. No heat is given off or required to make a phase change.

78) A precipitate is formed when a dilute solution of H_2SO_4 is added to

   A) Na^+
   B) K^+
   C) NH_4^+
   D) Al^{3+}
   E) Ca^{2+}

The correct answer is E:) Ca^{2+}. Most sulfate salts are soluble except $BaSO_4$, $PbSO_4$, and $CaSO_4$.

79) A sample of a vapor having a mass of 0.519 grams occupies 123 mL at 100° C and 745 mm Hg. What is its molecular weight?

A) 0.002 g/mol
B) 0.06 g/mol
C) 11.6 g/mol
D) 94.5 g/mol
E) 131.7 g/mol

The correct answer is E:) 131.7 g/mol. PV = nRT (745 mm)(1 atm/760 mm)(0.123 L) = (0.519 g / x mol)(0.082 L-atm/K-mol)(100 + 273 K) (0.121 atm-L)(x mol) = 15.87 g-L-atm   x = 131.7 g/mol

80) What is the molarity of a solution prepared by dissolving 1.96 g of Na_2CO_3 and diluting the solution to 100.0 mL?

A) 0.185 M
B) 0.196 M
C) 51 M
D) 0.298 M
E) 0.018 M

The correct answer is A:) 0.185 M. Molarity = number of moles of solute / number of liters of solution = (1.96 g Na_2CO_3)(1 mol Na_2CO_3/106 g Na_2CO_3) / 0.100L = 1.85 M

81) A student did a titration of 50.0 mL of CH_3COOH using 39.6 mL of 0.0950 N KOH. What was the normality of the CH_3COOH?

A) 7.52 N
B) 0.75 N
C) 7.52 x 10^{-2} N
D) 0.119 N
E) 1.20 N

The correct answer is C:) 7.52 x 10^{-2} N. $V_1N_1 = V_2N_2$ (50.0 mL CH_3COOH)(N_1) = (39.6 mL KOH)(0.0950 N KOH)
N_1 = 0.0752 N or 7.52 x 10^{-2} N

82) The Ksp of silver sulfide is 8 x 10-51. What is the silver-ion concentration of a saturated solution of silver sulfide?

   A) 1.00×10^{-17}
   B) 6.32×10^{-26}
   C) 2.00×10^{-17}
   D) 1.59×10^{-17}
   E) 6.32×10^{-17}

The correct answer is C:) 2.00×10^{-17}. $Ag_2S \leftrightarrow 2 Ag^+ + S^{2-}$ $K_{sp} = [Ag^+]^2 \times [S^{2-}] = 8 \times 10^{-51}$ OR Ksp = [Ag+]3 Therefore, the cube root of 8×10^{-51} is 2.00×10^{-17}.

83) What is NOT true of buffers?

   A) They take advantage of common ions
   B) They are derived from a weak acid and one of its salts
   C) A buffer solution can resist drastic pH changes
   D) Buffers are made of a weak acid and a weak base
   E) Buffer systems are at work in the human body

The correct answer is D:) Buffers are made of a weak acid and a weak base. All others are true of buffers.

84) The rate law for the reaction $CaCO_3 \rightarrow CaO + CO_2$ is

   A) $\Delta G = \Delta H - T\Delta S$
   B) $k[A]$
   C) $k[A]^a[B]^b$
   D) $[B]^b[C]^c/[A]^a$
   E) $k([B]^b[C]^c/[A]^a)$

The correct answer is B:) k[A]. A dissociation of one reactant gives a zero order rate law.

85) Triple point refers to the point at which

   A) The heat of vaporization, the heat of fusion, and the boiling point are equal
   B) A solid turns into a gas without becoming a liquid
   C) The heat of fusion equals the heat of vaporization
   D) Solid, liquid and gas are in equilibrium
   E) A plasma is formed

The correct answer is D:) Solid, liquid, and gas are in equilibrium. The triple point is the temperature and pressure at which solid, liquid and gas are in equilibrium.

86) The energy required to change 50 g of ice at – 25 C to steam at 100 C is

   A) 37.25 kcal
   B) 500 kcal
   C) 27.00 kcal
   D) 12.95 kcal
   E) 3375 kcal

The correct answer is A:) 37.25 kcal.
Heat 50 g of ice from -25°C to 0°C: (50 g)(1 cal/g°C)(25°C) = 1,250 cal = 1.25 kcal
Phase change 50 g ice to water at 0°C: (50 g)(80 cal/g) = 4,000 cal = 4.00 kcal
Heat 50 g of water from 0°C to 100°C: (50 g)(1 cal/g°C)(100°C) = 5,000 cal = 5.00 kcal
Phase change 50 g water to 50 g steam at 100°C: (50 g)(540 cal/g) = 27,000 cal = 27.00 kcal
50 g ice at -25°C to steam at 100°C: 1.25 kcal + 4.00 kcal + 5.00 kcal + 27.00 kcal = 37.25 kcal

87) It was found that 85.5 g of a nonelectrolyte dissolved in 1 kg of water lowered the freezing point of water 0.465 C. The molecular weight of the solute is

   A) 171 g/mol
   B) 342 g/mol
   C) 855 g/mol
   D) 85.5 g/mol
   E) 34.2 g/mol

The correct answer is B:) 342 g/mol. $\Delta T_f = K_f m$ 0.465° C = 1.86° C/m (m)   0.25 m = m = 0.25 mol/kg (85.5 g/1 kg)/(0.25 mol/kg) = 342 g/mol

88) What makes a hydrocarbon an alkene?

   A) All carbons have only single bonds.
   B) There is a double bonded carbon in the molecule.
   C) There is a triple bonded carbon in the molecule.
   D) There is more than one double bond in the molecule.
   E) There is an oxygen in the molecule.

The correct answer is B:) There is a double bonded carbon in the molecule. Alkenes have one double bonded carbon in the molecule.

89) The organic compound represented by CH3-COOH is

   A) An ether
   B) An aldehyde
   C) A carboxyl
   D) A ketone
   E) A hydroxide

The correct answer is C:) A carboxyl. A carboxyl has a double bonded oxygen and a hydroxide bonded to a carbon (COOH).

90) Name this organic compound:

$$\begin{array}{c} CH_2CH_3 \\ | \\ CH_3-CH-CH_2 \\ | \\ CH_2 \\ | \\ CH_3CH_2 \end{array}$$

   A) 2-ethylhexane
   B) 2-octane
   C) 2-ethyl-3-propylpropane
   D) 3-methylheptane
   E) 3-ethylhexane

The correct answer is D:) 3-methylheptane. It is a 7-carbon chain, heptane, with a 2-carbon methyl group on the third carbon.

91) F-C-ClBrH and F-C-HBrCl are called

   A) Isotopes
   B) Trans- and cis- isomers
   C) Geometric isomers
   D) Stereoscopic isomers
   E) Stereoisomers

The correct answer is E:) Stereoisomers. They are mirror images of each other.

92) In a reaction ΔH increases and ΔS increases

    A) The reaction cannot be spontaneous
    B) The reaction is endergonic
    C) The reaction can be spontaneous if the temperature is high
    D) ΔG will be positive
    E) The reaction could be spontaneous if TΔS > ΔH

The correct answer is E:) The reaction could be spontaneous if TΔS > ΔH. If ΔH increases (endothermic) and ΔS increases, the reaction is spontaneous only if the unfavorable heat content change is offset by a favorable entropy change.

93) What color is anhydrous CuSO4?

    A) Yellow
    B) White/Gray
    C) Blue
    D) Purple
    E) Black

The correct answer is B:) White/Gray. CuSO4 is copper sulfate. In its anhydrous form (when there is no water) it is white or light gray. However, when it is bonded with water (ex. CuSO4:5H2O) it becomes bright blue.

94) A 5.00-L flask, at 25° C, contains 0.200 mol of Cl_2. What is the pressure in the flask?

    A) 1.96 atm
    B) 4.89 atm
    C) 611.6 atm
    D) 0.979 atm
    E) 0.082 atm

The correct answer is D:) 0.979 atm. PV = nRT: (P)(5.00 L) = (0.200 mol Cl_2)(0.0821 L-atm/K-mol)(25 + 273 K) P = 4.89 L-atm / 5.00 L = 0.979 atm

95) The oxidation number of H in $Ba(OH)_2$ is

    A) +1
    B) -1
    C) +2
    D) -2
    E) 0

The correct answer is A:) +1. Hydrogen is always +1 except in a metal hydride such as NaH when it is -1.

96) The oxidation number of P in P_2O_5 is

    A) +2
    B) +5
    C) +10
    D) -5
    E) -10

The correct answer is B:) +5. If oxygen is -2 and there are 5 for a total of -10, then P must equal +10. There are 2 P, so each is +5.

Test Taking Strategies

Here are some test-taking strategies that are specific to this test and to other CLEP tests in general:
- Keep your eyes on the time. Pay attention to how much time you have left.
- Read the entire question and read all the answers. Many questions are not as hard to answer as they may seem. Sometimes, a difficult sounding question really only is asking you how to read an accompanying chart. Chart and graph questions are on most CLEP tests and should be an easy free point.
- If you don't know the answer immediately, the new computer-based testing lets you mark questions and come back to them later if you have time.
- Read the wording carefully. Some words can give you hints to the right answer. There are no exceptions to an answer when there are words in the question such as always, all or none. If one of the answer choices includes most or some of the right answers, but not all, then that is not the correct answer. Here is an example:

    The primary colors include all of the following:

    A) Red, Yellow, Blue, Green
    B) Red, Green, Yellow
    C) Red, Orange, Yellow
    D) Red, Yellow, Blue
    E) None of the above

    Although item A includes all the right answers, it also includes an incorrect answer, making it incorrect. If you didn't read it carefully, were in a hurry, or didn't know the material well, you might fall for this.
- Make a guess on a question that you do not know the answer to. There is no penalty for an incorrect answer. Eliminate the answer choices that you know are incorrect. For example, this will let your guess be a 1 in 3 chance instead.

 What Your Score Means

Based on your score, you may, or may not, qualify for credit at your specific institution. At University of Phoenix, a score of 50 is passing for full credit. At Utah Valley University, the score is unpublished, the school will accept credit on a case-by-case basis. Another school, Brigham Young University (BYU) does not accept CLEP credit. To find out what score you need for credit, you need to get that information from your school's website or academic advisor.

You can score between 20 and 80 on any CLEP test. Some exams include percentile ranks. Each correct answer is worth one point. You lose no points for unanswered or incorrect questions.

Test Preparation

How much you need to study depends on your knowledge of a subject area. If you are interested in literature, took it in school, or enjoy reading then your studying and preparation for the literature or humanities test will not need to be as intensive as someone who is new to literature.

This book is much different than the regular CLEP study guides. This book actually teaches you the information that you need to know to pass the test. If you are particularly interested in an area, or you want more information, do a quick search online. We've tried not to include too much depth in areas that are not as essential on the test. Everything in this book will be on the test. It is important to understand all major theories and concepts listed in the table of contents. It is also very important to know any bolded words.

Don't worry if you do not understand or know a lot about the area. With minimal study, you can complete and pass the test.

One of the fallacies of other test books is test questions. People assume that the **content** of the questions are similar to what will be on the test. **That is not the case.** They are only to test your "test taking skills" so for those who know to read a question carefully, there is not much added value from taking a "fake" test.

To prepare for the test, make a series of goals. Allot a certain amount of time to review the information you have already studied and to learn additional material. Take notes as you study, as it will help you learn the material.

Legal Note

All rights reserved. This Study Guide, Book and Flashcards are protected under US Copyright Law. No part of this book or study guide or flashcards may be reproduced, distributed or stored in a retrieval system, or transmitted in any form or by any means, electronic, mechanical, photocopying, recording, or otherwise, without the prior written permission of the publisher Breely Crush Publishing, LLC. This manual is not supported by or affiliated with the College Board, creators of the CLEP test. CLEP is a registered trademark of the College Entrance Examination Board, which does not endorse this book.

FLASHCARDS

This section contains flashcards for you to use to further your understanding of the material and test yourself on important concepts, names or dates. Read the term or question then flip the page over to check the answer on the back. Keep in mind that this information may not be covered in the text of the study guide. Take your time to study the flashcards, you will need to know and understand these concepts to pass the test.

Protons and neutrons are located where?	Atomic mass is also known as what?
The number of protons that an element has is known as what?	Which gases have the most stable outer electron configurations?
Inert gases are in what group?	Ionic size
Ionic size	Electronegativity

Atomic weight	Nucleus
Dmitri Mendeleev	Atomic number
8a	Noble gases
For an atom to attract electrons to itself in bonding	The radius of an ion measured from the center of the nucleus to the outermost electron

Single covalent bond	Coordinate covalent bond
Van der Waals forces are the weakest or the strongest?	Hydrogen bond
Network solids	Law of definite proportions
Ionic compounds	Molecular compounds

When only one of the atoms in a bond provides the pair of bonding electrons	Shared pair of electrons
Secondary bond between a partially positive hydrogen atom and a partially negative	Weakest
Elements in a compound always combine in the same proportion by mass	Substances in which all the atoms are covalently bonded to each other
Formed of covalently bonded atoms	Are formed using ions and use electrostatic charge and attraction

Law of multiple proportions	**Avogadro's number**
Gram atomic mass	**Gram formula mass**
Percent composition	**Kinetic theory**
Dalton's Law of Partial Pressures	**Boyle's Law**

6.02×10^{23}	Whenever two elements form more than one compound, the different masses of one element that combine with the same mass of the other element are in the ratio of small whole numbers
Mass of one mole of a compound	Of grams of an element that is numerically equal to the atomic mass in amu
Tiny particles in all forms of matter are in constant motion	Percent by mass of each element in a compound
At a constant temperature, the pressure of a gas will vary inversely with the volume	Gases in a single container all have the same volume and are at the same temperature, so the difference in their partial pressures is due only to the difference in the numbers of molecules present

Charles' Law	**Avogadro's Law**
Vaporization	**Amorphous**
Sublimation	**Triple point**
Aqueous solutions	**Solvation**

Equal volumes of all gases contain the same number of molecules such that V/n = constant (22.4 liters/mole)	At a constant pressure, the volume of a given amount of gas will vary proportionately with the temperature expressed in Kelvin
Solids that lack an ordered internal structure	Conversion of a liquid to a gas
The temperature and pressure at which solid, liquid and gas are in equilibrium	The phase change from solid to vapor without going through liquid
Occurs when those ions are surrounded by water molecules	Water samples containing dissolved substances

Henry's Law	Saturated solution
Molarity	Mole fraction
Raoult's Law	Amphoteric
Stoichiometry	Stoichiometry

Contains the maximum amount of solute for a given amount of solvent at a constant temperature and pressure	At a given temperature the solubility of a gas in a liquid (S) is directly proportional to the pressure of the gas above the liquid (P) such that $S_1P_2 = S_2P_1$
Number of moles of solvent divided by the combined numbers of moles of solvent and solute	Number of moles of solute / number of liters of solution
A substance can be an acid or a base depending on its circumstances	Vapor pressure of the solution is equal to mole fraction of the solvent times the vapor pressure of the solvent
Any reactant that is used up completely	Calculation of theoretical quantities associated with chemical equations

Endothermic reaction	**Exothermic reactions**
Calorimetry	**Entropy (ΔS)**
Le Châtelier's Principle	**Activation energy**
Rate-determining step	**Atom**

Give off heat as they occur, so have a negative change in heat ($-\Delta H$)	Takes heat to occur
A measure of the tendency of a reaction toward more disorder	Science of measuring heat
Minimum energy those colliding particles need to react	If a stress is applied to a system in a dynamic equilibrium, the system changes to relieve the stress
The smallest particle of an element	The step that is the slowest to happen

Shielding Effect	Entropy
Electronegativity	Polar molecule
Intermeiate	Hydrogen bond
Periodic Table of the Elements	Limiting reagent

A measure of the tendency of a reaction toward more disorder.	A decrease in attraction between an atom's nucleus and its outer electrons due to the electrons between the nucleus and outer electrons.
A molecule in which one end has a negative character and the other a positive character creating a dipole.	A measure of the tendency of an atom to attract electrons to itself in bonding.
A weak, secondary bond between a partially positive hydrogen atoms and a partially negative N, O, or F atom nearby.	A product of one reaction that immediately becomes a reactant in another reaction.
Any reactant that is used up completely in a reaction.	An organized table which groups and displays the elements according to various properties.

Octet rule	**Isotopes**
Intermolecular attractions	**Molar mass**
Molecular compounds	**Ionic compounds**
Organic compounds	**Electron Affinity**

Atoms of the same element (same number of protons) with different numbers of neutrons (making it charged).	Atoms are most stable with eight electrons in their outermost energy level, so atoms will either gain or lose electrons to attain that configuration.
Can be used in place of gram formula mass to refer to the mass of a mole of atoms or molecules or formula units of any element or compound.	Attractions which occur between molecules.
Compounds formed using ions and use electrostatic charge and attraction.	Compounds formed of covalently bonded atoms.
Energy change accompanying the addition of an electron to an atom to make a negative ion.	Compounds which contain carbon that is covalently bonded.

Ionization Energy	**Avogadro's Law**
Amorphous solids	**Miscible liquids**
Anions	**Cations**
Covalent bonding	**Molecular formula**

Equal volumes of all gases contain the same number of molecules.	Energy necessary to remove an electron from an atom to make an ion.
Liquids that are soluble in one another.	Lack an ordered internal structure and do not melt at a specific temperature.
Positively charged ions.	Negatively charged ions.
Shows the kind and number of atoms present in a molecule of a molecular compound.	Sharing of electrons to acquire a stable electron configuration to create a molecular compound.

Chemical Formula	**Molecular orbital**
Network solids	**Stoichiometry**
Condensation	**Vaporization**
Solvent	**Law of definite proportions**

Similar to atomic orbital, but created when two atoms combine and their orbitals overlap.	Shows the kinds and numbers of atoms in a formula unit of an ionic compound.
The calculation of theoretical quantities associated with chemical equations.	Substances in which all the atoms are covalently bonded to each other.
The conversion of a liquid to a gas (or vapor). Also called evaporation.	The conversion of a gas into a liquid.
The elements in a compound always combine in the same proportion by mass.	The dissolving medium.

Gram atomic mass	Mass number
Atomic number	Sublimation
Ionic Size	Atomic Radius
Molecule	Formula unit

The number of protons and neutrons in an element.	The number of grams of an element that is numerically equal to the atomic mass in amu.
The phase change from solid to vapor without going through liquid (ex. dry ice).	The number of protons in an element.
The radius of the atom measured from the center of the nucleus to the outermost electron.	The radius of an ion measured from the center of the nucleus to the outermost electron.
The smallest unit of an ionic compound.	The smallest unit of a molecular compound.

Melting point	Kinetic theory
Gram formula mass	Atomic mass unit (amu)
Atomic mass	Aqueous solutions
Dynamic equilibrium	Law of multiple proportions

The tiny particles in all forms of matter are in constant motion.	The temperature at which the solid turns into a liquid.
The unit used to measure the mass of protons (I amu) and neutrons (1 amu).	The total of the gram atomic masses multiplied by their subscripts in the formula of the elements.
Water samples containing dissolved substances.	The weighted average of the masses of the isotopes of an element. Also called atomic weight.
Whenever two elements form more than one compound, the different masses of one element that combine with the same mass of the other element are in the ratio of small whole numbers.	When the rate of evaporation equals the rate of condensation.

NOTES

NOTES

NOTES

NOTES

NOTES

NOTES

NOTES

NOTES

NOTES

NOTES

NOTES

NOTES

NOTES

NOTES

NOTES

NOTES

NOTES

NOTES

NOTES

NOTES

www.ingramcontent.com/pod-product-compliance
Lightning Source LLC
Chambersburg PA
CBHW081832300426
44116CB00014B/2562